About the Author

Richard currently resides in central Florida with his wife, Leigh-Ann, and his daughter, Hannah. He currently works for a mental health and substance abuse facility that is focused on providing help to first responders. When not at work or spending time with his family, he can be found running trails through his local forests and swamps in the brutal Florida heat.

Recovery Run: One Man's Journey from Rock Bottom to Ultra Marathoner

Richard Gallegos

Recovery Run: One Man's Journey from Rock Bottom to Ultra Marathoner

Olympia Publishers
London

www.olympiapublishers.com
OLYMPIA PAPERBACK EDITION

A CIP catalogue record for this title is
available from the British Library.

ISBN: 978-1-80074-792-0

Due to health privacy laws certain aspects of the emergency calls
found in this book have been slightly altered to maintain the strictest
patient confidentiality. This book contains graphic recounts of 911
emergency calls, drug and alcohol use, and suicidality. The content of
this book may not be suitable for all audiences.

First Published in 2023

Olympia Publishers
Tallis House
2 Tallis Street
London
EC4Y 0AB

Printed in Great Britain

Dedication

To my wife, Leigh-Ann, you are my best friend and my rock. Without you I would not be standing here today. To my daughter, Hannah, you are my motivation and inspiration to be a father you're proud of. To everyone out there struggling with mental health and/or substance abuse, keep your head up, and as difficult as it may seem, there is hope.

Acknowledgements

Thank you to my wife and best friend, Leigh-Ann Gallegos. You are the strongest, most compassionate, and amazing person I have ever met in my life. You believed in me even when I was incapable of believing in myself. You are my rock and the love of my life. Thank you to my daughter, Hannah, for being my inspiration and relentless motivation to continue being a father that you're proud of.

Introduction: Broken, Bruised and Boundless

"If you want to run, run a mile. If you want to experience a different life, run a marathon. If you want to talk to God, run an Ultra."

- Dean Karnazes

HOLY SHIT! God, please help me...what the HELL am I doing? I am so damn stupid... I am so damn stupid! God, if you just get me through this, then never again!

These were the words that I was desperately uttering through a steady flow of tears as the medic approached me at the mile eighty aid station at the iconic KEYS100. As he slid my shoes off and peeled my blood-soaked socks off my feet, I knew it was bad.

I could see the panic and disgust on my wife's face as she was standing over his shoulder, trying not to grimace at the sight of my wrecked feet. I saw my mom gasp as the medic lifted my foot to examine it.

Now would be a good time to let you know that at this point in my life, I had already worked many years as a paramedic, so there wasn't much that made me squeamish.

As I looked down, I didn't recognize the mess that was attached to my legs. My feet were glowing red and swollen beyond belief. The skin around each foot felt stretched and on the verge of splitting down the middle.

I took note of the painful pouches of fluid hanging off the side of my foot resembling extra deformed toes, and I studied the pulsating, stabbing pain they were sending up my leg. I noticed a loose flap of soggy white skin dangling between my toes. My entire foot was soft and pruned from the sweat that had collected in my shoe from the earlier twenty-four hours. The medic helping me compassionately referred to them as "FUBAR" (Fucked Up Beyond All Recognition).

After seeing the two disasters, the medic stated that he didn't think there was much he could do; I had let the blisters go for too long. He informed me that he would do what he could but made no promises of the outcome. After about forty-five minutes of torturous poking and prodding with needles and safety pins as I winced and squirmed in pain, he finally, with an exasperated sigh, informed me, "There's nothing more I can do. The blisters are too deep and the pads on your feet are too thick. I can tape them and hopefully they won't get any worse."

After hearing our exchange, the race marshal approached us and informed me that I was in dead last place. If I didn't get moving immediately, they would have to pull my race bib, which would result in immediate removal from the race. He hinted that if I was going to drop, now would be the time to do it. He tried to soften the blow to my pride and ease my decision by discussing how difficult this race was, especially for a first-time one hundred-mile run attempt.

Dropping was NOT an option. In the months leading up to the race, I made a resolution to myself, my crew, and anyone who would listen that quitting was NOT an option. I would either finish, run out of time or get carried away by an ambulance.

Since I still had time on the clock and the rescue wagon

was not called, I painfully crammed my bloody stump of a foot back into my sweat-soaked shoes and stood up.

I started by placing one painful foot in front of the other until I built up a pace that would make a snail laugh. Every step was torture; it felt as if the medic had filled my socks with Lego blocks or glass before placing them back on me. I could feel those drained sacs on my feet conspiring against me by sending incredible signals of pain to my already fried brain in a desperate attempt to incite panic.

YOU HAVE ANOTHER TWENTY MILES, YOU IDIOT... YOU CAN'T POSSIBLY THINK YOU CAN MAKE IT ON THESE FEET, my brain protested.

I limped about twenty yards beyond the aid station while openly sobbing. I was watching a year of training, dedication and focus slip right through my fingers.

It was at this point I started asking myself, *why*?

Why am I here?

I refocused on the road... Not the road in front of me but the road behind me. I started reflecting on my life and all the events that had brought me to this point. I remembered the depressing lows and suicidal thoughts that I had struggled with for so many years. After all, I have seen and dealt with some of the most heart-wrenching situations while responding to people in their darkest moments.

I remembered all the hell and self-hatred I endured while I looked in the mirror and despised the person who was looking back.

I remembered isolating myself into bathrooms to shoot opiates, because they helped me cope with the overwhelming anger and depression I was experiencing.

I remembered drinking liquor until my body would literally

reject it and my liver would scream in pain, all because I just wanted to be numb.

I remembered the look in my wife's eyes while she gazed upon me with tears forming and told me that she was no longer sure if she could stand by my side if I continued my kamikaze course.

I remembered all the agony I went through and what *real* suffering was.

Instantly, while standing in the blistering sun as vehicles whizzed by, surrounded by some of the most beautiful scenery this earth has to offer, I decided that I would no longer run out of desperation and fear but instead gratitude. After all, I had every reason in the world to be thankful...

Here I was, sober, happy, current physical pain aside of course, standing in a literal paradise and surrounded by the people that I love the most in this world, people who were loving enough to cram into a minivan for over twenty-four hours to crew me up to this point. Yeah, I might be in pain physically, but it was a welcome change to the many years I had spent as a numb, lifeless shell of myself.

I started to focus on all the things I was thankful for, and as I shifted my outlook on my current situation, my pace shifted as well. I went from a death march to a walk. From a walk to a shuffle. A shuffle to a trot and finally a trot to a full-on run. As my pace picked up so did my pain tolerance and optimism. Before long I felt as if I were flying.

It was during those unstoppable strides that I understood that even though I was broken and bruised, I was now boundless...

Chapter One

Part 1

Into Hell

"Dare to reach out your hand into the darkness, to pull another hand into the light."
- Norman B. Rice

It's around eleven p.m. The alarm and bell cut through the peaceful night air like a lightning bolt cast from Zeus himself. The sharp, sudden commotion penetrate you completely and shake you to your very core.

There is no warning, no build up, no polite, "Hey you're about to shit your pants". One moment you're drifting off to dreamland and the next your standing by your bedside, trying to figure out what's happening, and all the while your heart rate swears the end is near.

It only takes a microsecond to cast a person into a full fight-or-flight response. This is the same response you're faced with while jumping out of a plane, facing a boar eye to eye or receiving the "We need to talk" text out of the blue from your wife. It's a system-shocking bolt of adrenaline that will take you from zero to one hundred at the snap of your fingers.

You would think after being a paramedic for many years

that one's body and mind would adjust to the sudden and shocking calamity of emergency dispatch tones in the middle of the night, but I can tell you from experience, THEY DON'T!

After exactly 0.00025 seconds of utter confusion and panic, I realized what was going on and where I was. I was on shift, and we had a call.

As I stood next to my bunk, reaching for my boots in the now fluorescently lit room, I listened... I listened for the dispatcher to come over the radio and vaguely inform us of what we were being dispatched to. In my experience, 911 dispatchers try to get the emergency crew rolling then give them updates.

"Medic 35, Medic 35, we need you Code 2 for a reported motor vehicle accident."

Now, there is something I would like to make abundantly clear, and I know this may come as a shock, but not all 911 calls are an emergency.

As a matter of fact, I would venture to say most are not. It never ceases to surprise me the amount of people who will call for an emergency response because they have the hiccups, ingrown hairs, hangnails, minor constipation, mild toothaches and a plethora of other non-acute/non-emergent issues.

I've even responded to individuals who woke up from bad dreams and others who request pregnancy tests. Most, if not all, of these calls are considered a Code 2 response.

A Code 2 response was our radio speak for "non-emergent": this is something that dispatch can triage over the phone to determine if it is non-life threatening, and this type of response does not require the use of lights and sirens.

A Code 3 response, on the other hand, is something that is

deemed as an immediate emergency and requires a response involving lights and sirens along with urgent haste from the responding crew.

After learning the vehicle accident was a Code 2, I was able to bring the adrenaline high to a manageable level. I pictured a minor fender bender that would result in a quick medical exam and a patient refusal to transport.

BOY, WAS I WRONG IN THIS CASE!

As my EMT (Emergency Medical Technician) partner and I loaded into the ambulance and started to head towards the intersection reported, dispatch came over the radios and asked us to upgrade to Code 3, based on "new information" from the scene.

My partner, who was driving, glanced over at me and with a slight roll of his eyes sarcastically said, "Here we go…"

I keyed up the radio and asked for an update on the "new information" reported to dispatch to help me understand and visualize what we were about to roll up on.

I was met with a stern and abrupt, "STANDBY", from the dispatcher.

After about fifteen seconds of radio silence, our dispatcher started toning out and dispatching multiple other units to the same intersection that we were en route to. These units included multiple fire engines, a shift command officer and two other nearby ambulances.

Just as I was about to request an update for the second time, dispatch informed all responding units, "All units be advised: you are responding to a motor vehicle accident involving three vehicles. Witnesses report it as a high-speed collision and state one vehicle is smoking. There are multiple reports of entrapment and significant damage."

As I exchanged glances with my partner, we were both having the "Oh shit" moment that every emergency crew experience during their career. It's that moment when you realize that the call you originally thought would be a bullshit false alarm is actually like walking into hell.

Part 2

And Hell It Was

As we pulled up to the scene, I quickly realized that this accident was a lot worse than the witnesses had advised.

Our shift commander pulled up in his SUV and started surveying the scene moments before we arrived. After jumping out of our rig, I grabbed my equipment and ran over to my commander. Together we quickly formulated a plan of attack and started triaging patients.

Finding a life-threatening injury in this pile of twisted steel that once made up three separate vehicles was like trying to locate a mosquito in a swamp. It seemed like there were countless bodies involved, and everyone was teetering on the verge of death. The wreckage was so significant that we could not figure out what types of vehicles these individuals were in. All we knew was that we needed them out now!

The scene was unbelievable. It looked like a missile had struck the vehicles involved.

The accident consisted of three cars. Two of the cars were stopped at the red light, an SUV first in line and a mid-sized sedan behind it. While both vehicles patiently waited for the light to turn green, there was no way of knowing that an imminent threat was fast approaching. A third vehicle traveling at breakneck speed, roughly sixty to sixty-five miles per hour, did not see the red light or the vehicles stopped at it. Witnesses at the intersection stated that the driver smashed into the rear of the sedan without so much as tapping his brakes.

The impact sandwiched and crushed the middle sedan into the rear of the SUV, causing all passengers to be entrapped.

The impact pushed the SUV into the intersection, placing it on its side. All three vehicles were twisted together, like some type of abstract sculpture or special effects prop that you would see in an apocalyptic blockbuster.

After what felt like an eternity of waiting for support crews, when in reality it was maybe one to two minutes, the cavalry showed up.

We quickly got to work, cutting, pulling and prying contorted sheets of metal that were left over from vehicle doors, roofs and safety features.

As we extracted patients, we assigned a medic and support EMTs to treat them. We worked as efficiently as we could, given the circumstance of prolonged extraction. We operated as a single well-oiled entity, completing separate tasks in order to yield one needed outcome… extraction!

Each patient that was pulled out of the wreckage seemed to be worse than the last, if that was even possible.

The driver of the vehicle that caused the collision was obviously dead upon arrival. The injuries he sustained were completely incompatible with life.

At a certain speed, vehicles tend to crumple like a sheet of paper being prepped to be tossed into the garbage. Everything in front of the driver and passengers tends to end up on top of them, including the engine, transmission, dashboard and steering wheel. In this case, the steering wheel had crushed his chest and pinned him to his seat. Engine components were sitting in his lap, crushing his pelvis, abdomen and lower extremities. The hood, which was forced through the windshield, had split his skull and brain, causing immediate death.

For this poor soul, it was no longer a rescue attempt but a body recovery.

We turned our full attention to the patients who were still fighting and clawing to stay alive. As we cut through the wreckage with the Jaws of Life, we pried back the contorted and twisted hunks of metal. The remains resembled a sadistic onion that was being peeled layer by merciless layer.

As we made our way to the patient-filled center of the pile, we started to get a better idea of the injuries that we would be facing.

The carnage was unreal.

The driver, a middle-aged father, who was sitting in the once high-end supple leather driver's seat, was now pinned by the engine block and forced to sit as a front row witness to his own rescue attempt.

As we tore away the outside panels of the vehicle, we were able to visualize the profile of his legs. From the knee down they were twisted and crooked in multiple spots. At first glance they resembled a liquid state – both legs were snaked in and out of the tangled metal.

The steering wheel column was pressed into his pelvis, which made him securely trapped in his seat. The roof was bent down and inward, holding his head in a downward position, forcing his chin into his chest and making it difficult to supply enough oxygen per labored breath.

We tried to talk to him in an attempt to comfort him and let him know that we were here to help and we would have him out momentarily, but we may as well have been speaking in foreign clicks. The feeling of impending doom will prevent even the strongest minds from understanding basic information. Judging by the panic in his eyes, it was very obvious that he did not know what was going on around him.

His respirations increased significantly, and the once steady stream of blood that had been trickling out of his nose started to slide in and out of his nostrils with force, producing opaque blood bubbles that shone in the cool night air. It seemed that every movement we made to free him caused him even more immense pain. That pain was captured by the terror in his eyes and reciprocated by the fear in ours.

After approximately one and a half weeks in "trauma time", roughly ten to twelve minutes in standard time, we were able to free him from the steel fist of the wreck.

As we slid him out of the vehicle onto a backboard, we were able to get a first-hand account of the full scope of his injuries. It was so much worse than any of us could have anticipated. I don't think there was a single area of this man's body that went unscathed.

After strapping him to the backboard, we could see that he had multiple facial fractures, mainly to his cheeks and jaw. The swelling was unbelievable. If you didn't know you were looking at a human face, you would have had a hard time finding a landmark to distinguish it. As we cut his clothes off, we noted that he had a "flail segment": this is characterized as three or more rib fractures on the same side of the chest wall. This was easily determined due to the see-sawing motion his chest was making during every desperate breath.

His belly was hard and distended; the deep purples caused

by bruising made us believe that he had major internal bleeding. His pelvis was completely unstable and formless; it seemed that his pelvic bone was replaced with mush.

Both legs looked as if they had been rolled over by a bulldozer. Not only did they take on the formless shape of the pelvis, but they also had multiple open fractures with bone protruding. After securely strapping him to the backboard, we loaded him into an ambulance roughly twenty yards away. The treating medic and two extra EMTs jumped in the back, slammed the doors and they were off.

As I ran back to the pile of vehicles, I was able to survey the progress the individual crews were making. The driver and passenger of the SUV that was on its side were freed from the wreck and were on their way to the hospital with "critical injuries" unknown to me.

The passenger in the vehicle I was working on was free and in the process of being loaded up. She was the wife of the man whom I had helped free moments earlier. I didn't get a good look at her injuries, but I did notice that her treating medic was using a piece of equipment to provide artificial ventilations.

As I continued back to the warzone, it seemed as if everything was moving in slow motion as I heard my captain yell over all the loud equipment and generators, "There's a fucking kid back here!"

As I stepped back face-to-face with the now disassembled pile of debris, I witnessed a child, roughly five to six years old, being maneuvered out of the back of the vehicle.

He was unrestrained in the back seat at the moment of impact. He was forced onto the floorboard and pinned between the rear bench seat and the passenger seat. As the heavy rescue crew lifted the limp, lifeless-looking body, I knew I would be assigned this patient. I also knew his chances were very slim, based on the substantial mechanism of injury.

Once I was next to him, I quickly surveyed his injuries and instantly formulated a treatment plan and approach of attack.

He was completely unresponsive, and at the risk of sounding heartless, it was probably for the best, considering the extreme injuries he had sustained and the indescribable pain he would have felt.

In the world of emergency medicine, if a patient does not have a heartbeat or a clear and functional airway with respiratory drive, nothing else matters. As I nervously felt for a pulse, I found the faint metronome of a weak and thready heart. He was also still breathing on his own, short shallow breaths that resembled a guppy out of water, but breathing, nonetheless.

We used a piece of equipment called a bag valve mask, or BVM, to support his breathing and provide deeper, more fulfilling breaths. As I cut his clothing off to get a better idea of what I was dealing with, I was met with a horrific discovery: the same see-sawing chest rise and fall that his father had. I also noted multiple open fractures with protruding bones to both his arms and legs.

After securely strapping him to the backboard and taking every precaution to protect any underlying spinal injuries from becoming worse, we loaded him onto our stretcher. I jumped into the back of my ambulance and started prepping all the tools and equipment I would need to successfully negotiate his injuries.

We were off, flying towards the hospital as if our very own lives depended on it.

I started to frantically work on treating the most immediate life-threatening injuries. Seeing the extent of his trauma and knowing his breathing was not sufficient, I decided to intubate him. This consisted of inserting a tube into his airway that would allow us to take over control of his respirations adequately. After starting the IV, I dosed him with a sedative to keep him sedated and a paralytic that would help me advance the breathing tube past his gag reflex without the risk of him vomiting and aspirating. I inserted the tube and confirmed its placement. After a brief moment of internal celebration and a quick sigh of relief, we now had a secure airway and means to breathe for him.

As we flew down the quiet city streets, leaving nothing but a trail of flashing lights and a symphony of emergency sirens behind us, we did everything we could to stabilize the other injuries. I used needle decompression to help with the pressure that was building in his chest from the lung that was punctured by his broken ribs.

We stabilized all the fractures with bulky trauma dressing and monitored his cardiac rhythm and output very closely. His heart was weak but still fighting to pump life to his little broken body.

While nearing the hospital, I radioed ahead to give the unsuspecting trauma team a heads up of what to expect within the next five to eight minutes. I advised that I, Medic 35, was en route with a pediatric trauma alert (the highest acuity of injury a child can have) and a synopsis of all the injuries we were dealing with. I included in my report all medications that had been given and the fact that we were now breathing for this kid. I let them know the extent of the orthopaedic injuries that were sustained and the warning of a punctured lung.

Through an obviously stressed voice, the nurse on the other

end replied, "Copy, see you on arrival, Medic 35."

As we pulled up to the hospital, we were met by a trauma physician and two nurses, who came out to the ambulance bay to assist with the unload. As we briskly walked down the hall, I repeated my report to the physician, who was listening intently.

The hallway that led to the trauma bay in the emergency department was about thirty yards long but felt never ending.

As we approached and passed other people, they instinctively stopped in their tracks and hugged the wall to get out of our way. It was very obvious by the fast pace we were holding that every second counted for this little guy.

I watched as hallway onlookers tried to fight the urge to sneak a peek. Most quickly lost the battle and succumbed to their own curiosity. As they looked upon our stretcher, they grimaced and quickly averted their eyes.

As I glanced behind us, I noticed a steady trail of blood drops that were continuously dripping off our stretcher. I watched as people navigated the hallway as if they were walking gingerly through a minefield to avoid the small but consistent blood trail.

After reaching the trauma bay, we were met by about fifteen hospital workers. The team that met us consisted of two more physicians, multiple emergency nurses, emergency technicians, respiratory therapists, X-ray technicians, and even the chaplain. As we slid the child off our stretcher, the hospital team took over. The hospital staff looked like a robotic assembly line, every part moving in a precise and direct way towards a common goal – *to give this child every chance in the world to live!*

Part 3

Aftermath

After leaving the emergency room and making our way back down what now seemed a much shorter hallway, I noticed that the blood trail that we had left was gone and a "Wet Floor" sign had taken its place. There were people walking in both directions as they came and went, with absolutely no idea of the hell that had just passed through.

We made it to our ambulance. I looked at my watch, which showed that it was now about eleven forty-five p.m., roughly forty-five minutes after the initial call was dispatched.

I sat in the passenger seat writing my patient report, while my partner and the extra EMTs who rode in with us cleaned and prepped the back of the rig, preparing us for another call.

Before long, the back of our ambulance mirrored the tranquillity of the hallway, and unless you were privy to it, you would have never believed it was the stage for one of the darkest moments for a person, a child, nonetheless.

After arriving back at the station, I washed my arms and face, changed my blood-spackled uniform to a clean, fresh one and headed to my bunk room, removed my boots and sat on the edge of my bed. It was then that the realization of what I just participated in hit me like a speeding locomotive.

Sitting there, I felt a warm tear roll down my face and land on my lips. As I wiped away the salty sentiment, I pictured that kid playing with his friends at school, running around laughing, as my young daughter does. I thought about how he was too young and innocent to deal with this amount of hardship and how it wasn't fair for him to be going through this.

I could feel my sadness turn to anger and back to sadness over and over, the more I thought about him. I realized that there was no way in hell I was going to be able to sleep, so I decided to distract myself with some station chores.

I headed outside to wash the exterior of the ambulance, a task that needed to be completed every day, usually put off until the end of shift. As I approached the rig, I could see that it was already covered in suds. As I circled the lathered truck, I found my partner scrubbing it with a brush while listening to music with his earphones in. As he turned, he was startled by my presence. I could see by the red puffiness of his eyes that he had been crying as well.

He took out one ear bud and said, "Couldn't sleep either, huh?"

To which I replied with a flat, "Nope," as I picked up a wash brush to start helping.

As we both worked in unison to clean the truck, we both understood why we were outside washing a vehicle in the wee hours of the morning.

We were both trying to distract our minds from the call. That's what we do as first responders – we distract ourselves until our problems seem to fade away.

Unfortunately, the first responder field accepts a stigma that suggests, "If you ask for help, you're weak and not cut out for this job. We're the ones people call for help, not vice versa." Even though we never spoke about the call, we both understood the weight and impact the other felt.

After the truck was washed, it was a pretty uneventful night. My partner and I watched late night info T.V. while scrolling through our phones in an attempt to make time pass faster. Sleep was not an option, especially with our brains still running at one hundred miles per hour with images and thoughts of that little boy.

As the sun rose and the oncoming crew filtered in to relieve us, they asked if we were okay, because apparently we looked exhausted and beat up. We shook it off by saying, "Yeah, just a long night," as we gave a report and hand-off prior to leaving for home.

After arriving home, I sat in my car for a few minutes to conceal the weight of last night's shift. As I entered my front door, I walked past my three-year-old daughter's room. Peeking in, I saw Hannah asleep without a care in the world. My wife, Leigh-Ann, was up and ready to start her daily errand list, which began with grocery shopping on this particular day of the week.

She asked me how my shift was, and I just told her, "Challenging," as I reached for the Captain Morgan in my kitchen cabinet.

As the dark amber liquid flowed, the stiff smell of alcohol started to rise. I could see the concern on her face about my drinking. It's a look that grew more frequent over the years, especially with me reaching for hard liquor at eight a.m. I quickly diffused her concern by briefly describing the scene and the fact that I didn't sleep at all last night because *I couldn't turn my brain off.* Her face softened from a disappointed look to concern and understanding.

After pouring about two ounces into a coffee mug and tossing it back, I kissed her on the cheek and headed in to take a shower. As I stood in the hot water, I could picture my wife waking my daughter and preparing her breakfast. I knew it was only a matter of time before they headed to the grocery store and would be out of the house.

After about forty-five minutes, she entered the bathroom, which now resembled a steam room, and told me she and Hannah were off to the store. I stressed, *BE SAFE* and *I LOVE YOU.*

I could hear the garage door open then close as I turned off the water and quickly towelled off. I checked the garage and confirmed they had left, then I quickly made my way back to the kitchen as I felt a giddiness swell inside me.

I opened the cabinet and removed the bottle of Captain. I quickly grabbed the coffee mug I had used earlier and filled it to the rim. I downed the entire cup in about three gulps, filling my mouth completely each time.

As my eyes watered, my throat and chest burned from the poison. I pushed past the initial discomfort of desperation drinking, because I knew sweet relief from my mental freight train was just around the corner.

After engulfing the mug's contents in its entirety, I refilled the cup halfway and repeated. I anxiously replaced the liquor bottle in the cabinet, similar to how a child would put Christmas presents found prematurely back in their hiding place so as not to get caught red-handed.

As I made my way to the bedroom, I could feel the warm, calming embrace of the liquid relief fill me. I lay my head down on the pillow and reflected on the events of my day through my drunken twilight.

The details of the call started to fade, and the roller coaster of emotions started to plateau. I was able to turn my *brain off.*

As the alcohol soaked my grief-stricken mind, it made life a little lighter. At that time, I didn't reflect on the negative effects to my health, or the irony that I was indulging in the very thing that had caused the earlier accident or even the fact that this was a relationship that I had to indulge in behind my wife's back. All I focused on was the fact that once again the alcohol rescued the rescuer.

Or so I thought…

READER RESCUE – rumors have it that the little boy survived and was released from the hospital after dozens of surgeries and physical therapy. Rumors also say that his parents made it as well. While I still don't know the true validity of these rumors, I cling to them as truth.

Chapter Two

Part 1

In the Beginning

"I have great respect for the past. If you don't know where you've come from, you don't know where you're going."
- Maya Angelou

Looking at the road behind us is sometimes a painful process. It can bring to the surface memories and emotions that make us cry, cringe, become angry or freeze us in our tracks, all the while turning our stomachs inside out.

Although it is sometimes very difficult to locate and confront a lot of those dormant emotional landmines, I do believe it is one hundred percent necessary to put forth effort to heal wounds of the past, especially if you wish to successfully build resilience for the future.

If I were to think back to my childhood, I would be met mostly with memories of hot summer days, playing outside with my friends from sunrise until the street lights turned on, which signaled to all the neighborhood kids to drop what you're doing and hightail it home.

I pretty much lived outside as a kid and loved every minute of it. I spent my days playing basketball, football and running through the local woods while participating in "Man-hunt", our neighborhood's version of extreme "Hide-and-Seek".

I was never the most athletic or fastest kid. As a matter of fact, I was usually one of the last people chosen for any team sport. My short, stubby legs, coupled with my chubby stomach, made me a slow-moving liability for any team.

I loved almost everything about playing outside except running. Running was always a clear indicator of how much everyone else was better than me.

Being a fast kid made you superior to your slower-moving peers. Although I was never the best at games or sports, I loved taking part.

I have many happy memories from childhood, but I think my favorite is remembering the freedom from the crippling weight of adult responsibilities. On the surface I seemed like a happy, jovial kid, but there was already turbulence brewing from a young age.

At home, things were pretty "normal" growing up. I had two very hard-working parents who busted their backs so me and my younger brother, David, could have better than they had growing up.

Looking back on it, I'm not sure how my parents made their just-above-minimum-wage jobs provide so much. I lived in a small house in a quiet neighborhood, surrounded by a quickly deteriorating side of Orlando.

Our house was usually jam-packed with family members. We housed anywhere between seven to ten individuals at any given time: aunts, uncles and adult cousins made up the mix.

The home was owned by my grandmother from my mom's side, whom I affectionately referred to as Nana. She was the

33

matriarch of the family, and what she spoke translated to law. She loved God and her family above all else. She would give anything she had to provide for her family, and although she continuously poured love onto her entire family, I always knew I was her favorite.

My Nana and I spent the majority of our time together. She was my primary caregiver, since both of my parents had to work to make ends meet. She was one of the sweetest ladies in the world, always ready to issue a hug and an encouraging word. She instilled many of my morals and faiths, both in God and in humanity.

My mother and father loved my brother and me very much and did their very best to exceed all of our needs and wants. We had new bikes, new toys, new clothes, newly released video gaming systems and family vacations every year.

My parents, mostly my mom, made sure we didn't go without. My father was forced to take a more passive role due to all the different personalities and opinions on how us boys should be raised.

My aunts felt more entitled to give parental input than he did. Unfortunately, my mother would always side with her sisters and her mother to overrule my father at almost every opportunity.

Our happiness was her number one goal in life, even if that meant not providing the much-needed discipline, open communication and structure a growing child needs. She was a good mom, not the easiest to talk to, but good, nonetheless.

Early childhood was pretty standard and unremarkable. I have so many pleasant memories that any sadness is completely diluted. It wasn't until I hit middle school that I started to realize how relentless and cruel the world could be.

Part 2

Sticks and Stones

Author Kamand Kojouri once said, "Some people are in such utter darkness that they will burn you just to see a light. Try not to take it personally."

For me growing up, there was no place darker than the hallways of my middle school. It seemed that the bullies who patrolled those halls found new ways to set me ablaze every day.

Middle school is a very difficult time for most, with a wide range of raging hormones, awkward physical growths, cracking voices and immature behaviors. It's no wonder most of us look back at that time of our lives and cringe.

For me however, this period presented more challenges than your typical teen years. For reasons unknown to me, I somehow ended up on the radar of my school bullies.

My tormentors consisted of about eight juvenile terrors led by one single hateful head. He controlled this group like a general controls a platoon of foot soldiers. I never understood what I ever did to make them hate me so much, and I probably never will. All I know is that they used me as an outlet to air out all their pent-up aggression and frustration.

I became a target early on in sixth grade and carried that mantle until I graduated eighth grade. Every school day was stressful and scary. The abuse manifested as a wide range of psychological and physical torment. It was almost impressive how inventive they were in developing new forms of intimidation and embarrassment to try on me. There are so many negative memories from my middle school era that I'm hard pressed to find any happy ones.

I can remember scrambling from the school bus to my classroom so as to not bump into the General or his platoon of miscreants. While most kids were gathered socializing, I was planning my route of evasion. I planned each step of my brisk scurry with purpose. I learned their morning routine and took every precaution to avoid stepping into their line of sight. I would peek around corners and check my blind spots continuously to make sure I wasn't being stalked or set up.

On the days that my planned sidestepping was less than perfect and I would somehow catch their attention, I knew one thing... *it's going to be a long day.*

My memory is littered with scenes of basketballs, footballs, dodge balls and pencils being bounced off my head as I would pass the platoon. Memories of being spit on, pushed to the ground and tripped while walking are other common reflections.

Among all the various nightmares I recall making up my middle school experience, one in particular always seems to stick out.

It was fall of my seventh-grade year, and it had already been an exhausting couple of months since school had started. As my bus pulled into our middle school and prepared to unload the wave of loud, obnoxious teens and preteens, I knew today's evasion strategy needed to be adjusted to consider the early-morning thunderstorms that were conspiring against me.

Didn't the weather know that the sudden downpour would force everyone who would typically congregate in the outside courtyard into the indoor hallways for shelter?

Just as I frantically accepted that I didn't have control of the situation and I would need to modify my objective and approach, I was forced off the bus by the free flow of unloading children, similar to a weak swimmer being swept from the safety of the shallows by a rip current.

I found myself standing directly outside the bus in the pouring rain, trying to gather my bearings. I'm sure if I could have seen the look in my eye, it would have resembled that of a soldier who had just parachuted behind enemy lines and needed to make a quick survey before instinctively choosing a direction and path to safety.

I quickly entered the building and wiped the rain off my arms. The freezing air conditioning penetrated me and heightened my senses.

I made my way cautiously down the packed hallway, keeping a keen eye out for the enemy. The hallway that held my first period classroom was about fifty yards long and was likened to a cattle drive, with students squeezing past one another in hopes of making it to their first-period class before the bell rang.

I could see my classroom and my teacher standing directly outside, ushering the wet kids along the humid walkway. I knew if I could make it to the safety of her line of sight, I would be home free. As I dug in and pressed through the crowd, I kept my eyes locked on her. I focused on her with the same intensity as a football running back would focus on the goal post.

Approaching the classroom, my teacher and I locked eyes. She smiled and greeted me. I entered the safety of my classroom and made my way to my desk. After setting my backpack down and taking out a now soaked version of last night's homework, I sat in my seat and awaited the start of the day's lesson.

As I started to let my guard down, I could feel a tingling pressure in my bladder. I'm not sure if it was my nerves or the mixture of rain and air conditioning, but either way I had to use the restroom and use it badly!

Now, there was no way in hell I was exiting my classroom before the first bell. That would be too risky, and I didn't want to gamble running into any undesirables in the hallway.

After the morning announcements, the Pledge of Allegiance, and the homework was collected, I asked my teacher for the restroom pass. She told me to hurry, because she would be starting to cover new material momentarily; I didn't have the best track record for being a student who could understand material without maximum instruction.

I grabbed the hall pass on my way out of the door and made my way to the restroom with deliberation. I made it to the restroom just in time. I entered the door and scoped out a urinal in the unoccupied boys' room. It felt like my bladder was exploding.

As I stood there relieving myself, I heard the squeaky door to the restroom open. I glanced over and felt a shiver of instant panic take over. I was face-to-face with the General himself. It took him a moment to realize who he was looking at, but once he figured it out, his brow furrowed. I quickly zipped my pants up and prepared.

He acknowledged me by saying, "Good morning, fag!"

I quickly looked down and tried to make my way out of the now bully-blocked door without making too much eye contact.

He approached me and squared his much larger body up with mine and repeated, with even more force this time, "I

SAID, GOOD MORNING, FAGGOT!"

Through a very shaky and cracking voice I said, "C'mon, I just need to get back to class," while my eyes filled with tears.

He quickly pushed me backwards with a jolt. My back slammed into the wall, forcefully pushing the timid air out of my lungs. The General stepped forward as the back of my head bounced off the blue tile wall.

He leaned down about two inches to look me in the eye and ask, "What's wrong, PUSSY? You look like you want to cry."

At that moment, my brain lost its ability to form words or logic. I just kept stuttering, "I need to get to class," while trying to maneuver myself past him.

He continued to block my exit. His relentless barrage of insults was strung together almost poetically. They penetrated me even deeper than the cold air of my school. All I could do in the moment was release a steady stream of tears that acted like kerosene to a fire.

He saw the control he had over me and became drunk with power.

He continuously pushed and bounced me off the cold wall while mushing my face with the palm of his sweaty hand. To be honest, I'm not even one hundred percent sure that his palms were sweaty; it may have just been the tears that transferred off my face.

I tried to find a "happy place" but was mentally frozen in the moment by the torment

After pushing me into the wall for the fourth or fifth time, my legs finally buckled. I slid down the cold wall to the floor as my shirt rolled up, exposing my pudgy, pale stomach. I tried desperately to cover my stomach and lift myself up off the urine-covered floor, as it saturated my jeans.

Once I had lifted myself halfway to my feet, my intimidator swept my feet from under me, bringing me crashing back down to the cold, wet, piss-soaked floor.

He ordered me to, "STAY DOWN, FAT BOY!"

I felt so powerless as I sat there soaking up all the waste in my immediate proximity. All I could do was focus on his shoes, because any eye contact may have been interpreted as a challenge and anger him further.

As I started to surrender to the feeling of impending doom, another student entered the bathroom. I moved intuitively, seizing my moment while the General's attention on me was briefly broken.

I lunged myself into the handicap stall and locked the door. After two or three attempts to shake the door open, he retreated.

As he was leaving the bathroom he announced, "I'll see ya later, fag!"

I began to cry again as I sat behind the still-locked bathroom stall and tried to collect myself. I quickly took my pants off and wiped my piss-dampened thighs with the rough generic brown paper towels.

I sat on that porcelain throne of loneliness for the rest of the day, frozen in fear. I could hear boys coming and going as they talked and laughed without a care in the world.

Like Pavlov's dog, every time I heard the faint squeak of the bathroom door, I reacted. Only for me, the reaction wasn't salivating in anticipation of a treat: it was complete and utter stillness brought on by a primal fear welling from within.

As the minutes turned into hours, I sat there with nothing to do. This was long before the era when every child had a cell phone and a world of entertainment at their fingertips.

I sat there and daydreamed to distract myself from the molasses-like pass of time. I daydreamed about being home and playing my Nintendo 64 or being outside shooting basketball with neighborhood friends. For brief moments, my sadness was replaced with reprieve. I pictured being brave enough to stick up for myself and what it would be like to no longer live in fear.

However, the longer I sat there, the angrier and more insidious my thoughts became. I would fantasize about what it would be like to be able to bully the General in the same manner he pushed me around.

I daydreamed about making his life a living hell and him sitting in the boys' room, completely isolated. I could feel the anger inside bubble up and fill me. It was a disheartening feeling and I could tell that I wasn't built to hold on to this type of anger.

There was nothing I could do with it anyways: I was too chicken to actually stand up for myself and scared of what that would result in, most likely, an epic beat down.

The hours passed by, and soon the afternoon announcements came over the school's PA system. I knew this was my chance to free myself from my sewage-scented prison.

I darted out of my stall and back into the hallway. I scampered to the exit of the building that was adjacent to the bus loop. I didn't care that I was leaving my backpack behind or the fact that my mom would be getting a call from the school that would inform her of my absence. All I cared about was getting on my bus with no further conflict.

I made it outside and approached my bus. I surprised my driver by knocking on the door to enter. She was reading the newspaper, and you could tell she wasn't expecting kids so soon. As she swung open the folding bus door, I stepped aboard. It was the first time all day that I felt relieved.

She asked with a chuckle, "You in a hurry to get home or something?"

I replied, "Yes, ma'am, you have no idea."

I made my way to the back of the bus and took a seat. The worn out faux leather was a welcomed change to the hard plastic toilet seat that I had spent the entire day sitting on.

As the other students loaded onto the bus, I sat quietly with my head pressed against the window, looking out. I reflected on the day and everything I had been through.

Even though I tried to look at it from every perspective, I couldn't figure out what I ever did to deserve that type of treatment. I couldn't figure out *why*. During the entire ride home, I was surrounded by the chatter and commotion of my peers, but I still felt utterly alone.

I knew that even though I had managed to live to fear another day, it was only Monday, and if I had learned anything from my middle school experience so far, it was that history tends to repeat itself, and in my case it repeated to some extent almost every day.

Part 3

The End of an Error

After three years of consistent, innovative, physical and psychological torment, I approached the end of my middle school career. I knew that the group of bullies that made my life a living hell would be pouring into a different high school, and I rejoiced at the fact that I would most likely never see them again. I looked forward to the next chapter of my young life. I knew that high school would provide some much-needed relief from the immature bullies that I had struggled with, *wouldn't it?*

As the last day of eighth grade came to an end, I loaded onto my middle school bus one last time. I gazed at the school as we departed and wondered, *how many others would be setting foot onto a battleground instead of a middle school next school year?*

How many others would hate coming to school because of the peer-cultivated hellish atmosphere?

How many others would come face-to-face with the enemy known as "the school bully"?

As the school disappeared behind the surrounding trees during our departure, I turned my eyes to the road ahead. I pictured walking into a brand new school with brand new people and a brand new slate to reinvent myself upon.

While I anxiously daydreamed about what was to come, my weary and cynical mind kept me in check. I asked myself, *what if high school is the same as middle school?*

What if I'm met with the same type of psychological torture?

How could I deal with another four years on the battlefield?

As I struggled to get my cynicism under control, I refocused my thinking back to the positives. I told myself that I would have an entire summer to reinvent myself and become the person I wanted to be in high school.

After arriving home, I went to my room and started thinking of the ways I wanted to recreate myself. I knew that I wasn't a tough kid, and the lack of structure in my upbringing taught me to quit anything if it started to get too hard.

I also knew that I was overweight, and this was a huge contributor to my low self-esteem. You see, I come from a long family line of hefty people, and happily I had followed suit.

I spent the summer formulating and executing my plan to improve the areas of my life that I found problematic, mainly my weight. I started to play outside more and more, finding a direct correlation between physical activity and weight loss. As the pounds started to shed, I discovered an even more crucial connection between my physical activity level and my self-esteem. The more I moved, the better I felt about myself.

I continued to work hard over the entire summer, learning to discipline myself and hold myself accountable.

As the long summer days came to an end, I found a new person in the mirror looking back at me. I was proud of this person, not only because he was thinner and healthier, but because he had achieved a goal that he had worked so hard towards.

I learned one of the most important life lessons that

summer…

The feeling of self-worth that you achieve in setting goals, working towards them, and reaching them gives you a feeling unlike any other.

For the first time in my life, I was proud of myself. I decided to let that timid little boy stay in middle school. I made a resolution that summer to walk into high school as a confident young man… and that is exactly what I did.

READER RESCUE – I should have talked to my parents or teachers about my bullies. I was just so terrified that it would make my time in that school so much worse. My mother, as loving as she was, communicated best by yelling, not that she was angry, it was just her resting tone. I didn't have the safety net of open communication in my house. I was never taught how to talk about my emotions or feelings. If I'm being brutally honest, I was also scared to admit weakness and loss of control. I grew up in a time where standing up for yourself meant you were on your own, or at least that is how I interpreted it.

Chapter Three

Part 1

Laws of Attraction

"A soulmate is the one person whose love is powerful enough to motivate you to meet your soul, to do the emotional work of self-discovery, of awakening."
- Kenny Loggins

After many years of preteen torture during my middle school years, I finally found sanctuary in high school. I'm not sure if this feeling of relief and foreign sense of pride was because I lost my childhood pudge, mended a cracking voice, grew about three inches, had my orthodontic braces removed, and/or the fact that I now had testosterone coursing through my veins, but I think it was mostly because I walked a little taller since I had started to like myself.

No matter the reason, I just felt relieved that I was met with a blossoming social life and acceptance from my peers.

I was loving school, and I looked forward to attending every day. My grades, which usually only allowed me to pass by the skin of my teeth, began improving considerably, and my schoolhouse fears slowly drifted away.

I had no idea that my life could improve so quickly and so

drastically. By the end of my tenth grade year, I felt unstoppable: I had a large group of friends and no significant issues in my life. My self-esteem, that I earned from exercising, continued to increase and develop.

Everything was trending in the right direction. Little did I know that my life was once again going to be turned upside down, only this time for the better.

Now, there are times in a person's life when their breath is simply taken away by beauty. The person struggles to comprehend anything in the moment, and all they know is that everything seems right in the world.

These times are usually experienced while gazing upon a sunset at the Grand Canyon for the first time, watching a sunrise over a crystal clear, salty coastline or finding a wildflower-covered path through a beautiful mountainside. For a brief moment, the person is completely isolated by raw, uncut beauty and feels as if everything is going to be okay.

I believe that most people think that you need to travel to isolated, exotic, and untampered regions to capture such a breath-taking view. For me, it was as simple as attending my summer school Drivers' Ed. course, which took place in the back parking lot portables of my outdated high school, between my sophomore and junior year.

It was June 2, 2003. I was sitting at my desk, in the mothball-scented portable that housed my summertime course. I was looking around, trying to figure out who to befriend and spend my time with; after all, we would be in the same class Monday to Friday from seven a.m. to two p.m.

It was your typical early morning high school scene, with some kids hanging around the class socializing, while others were in dreamland with their heads on their desks. I scoped out a few people whom I was acquainted with and that I knew well enough to comfortably approach during down time.

It was about three minutes after the bell rang when *she* walked in. It was obvious she had had a rough morning by the annoyed and serious look on her face. I could tell she did not like being late, even if it was only by a few minutes. Even through the frustration, she glowed with radiance. The entire world slowed, the lights dimmed and the 1980s hit song "(I Just) Died in Your Arms Tonight", by Cutting Crew, played in my head.

I don't remember anything that was taught during that first day of Driver's Ed. All I knew was, SHE… WAS… GORGEOUS!

I was captivated, I was stricken… I WAS IN TROUBLE!

I spent much of that morning trying not to get caught staring at her. She was amazing, and the best part, she was friends with people that I knew as well. I had my in! Now, I just needed to come up with the perfect smooth introduction.

Our class was broken into two different sections: classroom lessons and driving lessons. During the driving lessons, the class would go outside to the outdoor bleachers that surrounded the driving course. During the times you were not driving, you could openly socialize with the other students awaiting their turn to show what they had behind the wheel.

I made sure to be one of the first people out of the door when it came time for us to head to the bleachers. I had to be sure to set myself up so that I could be in the same proximity of this angel.

After strategically placing myself, I saved seats for that group of friends. As they all trickled up to the bleachers, she followed suit.

There I was, sitting just a couple of feet away, with her perfume lingering under my nose. I went over about one hundred different slick introductions that would make me look cool and debonair.

I finally talked one of my friends into making an introduction, then I would pick up the conversation and sweep her off of her feet. There's nothing like the confidence of a fifteen-year-old boy… right?

My friend got her attention and introduced me. As she focused her eyes in my direction, instantly I lost all ability to formulate words. Every bit of saliva in my mouth dried up and my tongue turned into a mixture between sandpaper and the Sahara Desert. I felt my pulse quicken and at the same time my brain forgot to breathe. I quickly lost every charming intro that I had practiced over and over in my head.

"My name's Richard," is what barely fell out, as I internally choked for air.

"I'm Leigh-Ann," she responded in the sweetest voice.

There was a brief, awkward silence that needed to be filled. I was so swept up by her beauty that all I could do was compliment her. I searched for the right words but fell short.

"How do you get your eyelashes so long?" is what fumbled out of my bone-dry mouth.

She giggled and played it off before returning to her conversation with her friends.

I knew I had to do better.

Over the next three weeks, I worked on getting and keeping her attention. We started to develop a friendship and would frequently sit next to each other. We would talk about topical subjects: family, friends, background and other luke-warm topics.

We would share each other's early-generation Nokia phones, playing "Snake" and other primitive cellular games.

As the end of the summer term quickly approached, I knew I needed to speed my progress up. The more we spoke, the more I wanted to learn about her. She was amazing, smart, charming and beautiful. I didn't want to go the remainder of the summer without speaking to her.

On the last day of summer school, I asked her to meet me after class. I thought this would be the perfect time to ask for her phone number. Unfortunately, she misunderstood me and was not there as I anxiously exited the classroom.

Luckily, I had one of her best friends' phone numbers. I reached out and asked if she could give me Leigh-Ann's contact. To my surprise, she was with Leigh-Ann, out to lunch.

I awkwardly and embarrassingly held the line while she asked permission to give out Leigh-Ann's number. She came back on the line again with Leigh-Ann's blessing, and just like that… I had her number!

I called Leigh-Ann later that night and we briefly spoke. I told her how happy I was to be able to speak to her and that I would call her in a week after I got back home from my family's summer vacation. She told me that she was looking forward to it.

I WAS ON CLOUD NINE FOR THE REST OF MY VACATION!

After arriving home, I called her, and we spoke for hours. I told her that I had a crush on her and asked her out on a date. She told me that she needed to get to know me a little better before agreeing to a date, but she did sound excited at the prospect.

I spent the next two weeks pouring my heart out on the phone. I talked about every aspect of my life and got to know every aspect of hers. We would fall asleep on the phone and wake up to the annoying repetition of the off-the-hook dial tone of the archaic landline. After baring every aspect of my life, I finally felt that she knew me well enough to make an informed decision. So, I asked her to be my girlfriend again, and this time I was met with a cheerful "Yes". That night, we agreed on meeting at the movie theater at a local mall, so that our parents could meet, before walking into the theater to watch *2 Fast 2 Furious* – her choice.

As we entered the movie theater, my heart was pounding out of my chest the entire time. I finally worked up the courage to extend my hand to hold hers. She met me halfway, and we interlocked fingers. It was like holding hands with an angel. I was beside myself, floating with happiness. This was the start to something magical. To this day, that night is one of my favorite memories.

Part 2

Gravity

Leigh-Ann and I were inseparable throughout the rest of high school. She brought out the very best in me. I wanted to be a better person, because she deserved the very best version of me. I loved her so much, and for reasons unbeknownst to me, she returned the feeling. She was my everything, my best friend and the person that my young heart wanted to spend the rest of my life with.

Lao-Tzu once said, "Being deeply loved by someone gives you strength, while loving someone deeply gives you courage."

Leigh-Ann gave me the inspiration and determination that I needed to devote myself to school and graduate. I always assumed that I would drop out, because that's what everyone in my family did. I assumed that I would be breaking my back for the same company everyone else in my family worked for.

Leigh-Ann had a way of inflating me while at the same time keeping me grounded. She was brilliant, one of the top students in our class, and she believed in me!

After two years in a continuous committed relationship, we graduated high school together. It was one of the proudest moments of my life. I was the first in my family to ever graduate high school, and this was a huge step for me, *but* I was filled with overwhelming thoughts of, *what now?* I was floating adrift in unknown waters. I was never prepared for this step in life. All I knew was that if Leigh-Ann was by my side, I could face anything.

After two wayward years in and out of college, there were still many unknowns in my world.

What are you going to do with the rest of your life?

What are you passionate about?

What can you picture yourself doing for a living?

The only thing that stood steadfast was my unyielding love for Leigh-Ann. I didn't have any plan for the future, but I knew I wanted to spend every minute of it with her.

At this time, I was working with the developmentally disabled in a physical management department. My job was basically assisting physically disabled people out of their wheelchairs so that they weren't in the sitting position all day. Aside from the incredibly low pay, it was a decent job, but it wasn't something I wanted to spend the rest of my life doing. Leigh-Ann was working in the medical records department at a local hospital while attending college.

I spent almost every minute thinking of Leigh-Ann while working. I couldn't wait to see her every day when our shifts were over. One of the worst times of the day was when we had to depart for the night. I was living with a friend in an apartment across town, and she was still living at home with her parents and younger high school-aged sister.

One evening, after departing for the night, it finally dawned on me.

YOU LOVE HER, YOU FOOL!

IT DRIVES YOU CRAZY TO BE AWAY FROM HER.

MARRY HER, YOU IDIOT...

Boom, the seed was planted. I was determined to marry the woman I loved; I was determined to marry my best friend.

I saved up to put a very modest ring on a layaway plan. Once I finally paid it off, I was unstoppable. I would fantasize about living out the rest of our lives together and starting our own family; it's something we talked about frequently over the years.

I decided to follow the traditional route of asking for her parents' blessing before proposing. Her parents were divorced, and her mother was remarried, so I had two sets of parents to sit in front of.

This didn't bother me in the least. I knew her parents loved me, and they knew that we had been in a committed, loving relationship for four years, so they would probably be expecting it. Man, oh man, was I wrong.

After calling her father to set up a time to sit down, I was told, "I think I know what you want to talk about, and I don't want to have that conversation. I suggest you rethink your decision."

Defeated, I got in my car and drove over to her mother's house to sit with her and Leigh-Ann's stepfather.

After explaining that my intention was to marry Leigh-Ann, her mother broke down and cried tears of sadness and opposition. You could tell that she did not want me to propose and was very vocal about her disapproval.

Her stepfather looked at the ring, then back at me, and then quickly exited the room to the garage. This was the last time he spoke to Leigh-Ann and I for months.

Her mother looked devastated as I left. I sat in my car for a few minutes wondering why all of sudden I was being met with such discouragement.

Maybe it was because I didn't have a high-paying job or an exact plan for success.

Maybe they wanted Leigh-Ann to finish school first and start a career.

Maybe, deep down, they were hoping Leigh-Ann would realize that she was out of my league and decide to move on.

No matter the reason, I knew one thing: I loved Leigh-Ann more than anything else in life, and I knew I wanted to marry her. I also knew she felt the same way.

I proposed later that night and was met with a loving, excited, "YES". I slid the ring on her trembling finger, and we were engaged!

When Leigh-Ann arrived home, she was hoping to share her excitement with her mother, but unfortunately, she was met with the same discouragement that I had experienced earlier.

We decided that we wouldn't let any opposition or tears of sadness rob our joy. We planned our VERY humble and modest wedding with maximum emotional support from my family and little to no support from hers.

Seven months after the proposal, our wedding day arrived, and I found myself standing at the altar celebrating the happiest moment of my life.

Leigh-Ann and I went on to be the stereotypical poor newlywed couple. These were some of the best years of my life. We never allowed our lack of funds to come between us. The struggle became the welding that held us together. We overcame adversity and grew so much deeper in love. It almost seemed that every day I fell deeper and deeper in love. She was my world, and the love between us served as my gravity.

Part 3

Love^2

A year and a half into my amazing marriage and beautiful financial struggle, I finally figured out what I wanted to do with my professional life.

I decided that I would become an emergency medical technician (EMT) then continue on to be a paramedic. As usual, Leigh-Ann was right there behind me to offer her love and support. School was never my strong point, but Leigh-Ann truly believed in me, even when I didn't believe in myself.

I was terrified of failure. My track record of giving up when things become difficult ran deep. I knew this was a huge endeavor I was undertaking, but with her in my corner I enrolled into my local state college's EMT program.

All my insecurities towards schoolwork came rushing back. However, this time was different, because now I had a wife at home to provide for. I sunk my heels into the ground and studied my ass off. I passed my coursework with straight As and was awarded my EMT license. I used that license to start my career in emergency medicine.

I was offered a position at a private ambulance company in Orlando that mainly provided interfacility transport from nursing homes. It was not a glamorous job, but it served its purpose while I attended paramedic school.

This was an extremely stressful time in my life between

work and school, and I didn't have time to take care of myself. I ended up gaining around sixty to seventy pounds due to the emotional stress-eating and the lack of time for exercise. While my weight was resting on my waistline, the weight of the world rested on my shoulders.

I learned early on that I didn't know how to process and cope with stress. As mentioned, my upbringing taught me to quit anything when it became challenging, and as much as I wanted to quit now, I knew I wouldn't just be letting myself down but also my wife. If my ingrained coping skills weren't weak enough, I was also smoking a pack of cigarettes a day in hopes it would help me cope with the stress.

Life is funny, in a way. Just when you think that you can't handle any more, life turns around and says, here's the cherry.

Now, I can tell you exactly where I was when I received the most important phone call of my life. I was at work, sitting in the passenger seat of the ambulance, stuck in traffic in downtown Orlando, returning to my station after dropping a patient off at the hospital.

My wife called, and when I answered, her voice was giddy and filled with excitement. She asked how my day was going and in the middle of my response, she busted out by saying, "WE'RE PREGNANT!"

I dumbfoundedly responded, "What?"

She reiterated, "We're pregnant!"

I have never been so blindsided by overwhelming happiness in my life! I scared my partner with a sharp burst of celebration. I told Leigh-Ann that I would head home as soon as I got back to the station. I called one of my buddies, who was known for his willingness to pick up spur-of-the-moment overtime. He agreed to meet me at the station, and then I was off.

Upon arriving home, I busted through the door like a S.W.A.T. team of one. I wrapped my arms around Leigh-Ann, and we both sat on our couch crying tears of joy. We knew that our life was going to take a drastic turn for the better, if that was even possible.

I continued to work as an EMT, picking up as much overtime as my school schedule would allow, in preparation for being a father. Leigh-Ann and I always talked about her being a stay-at-home mom after giving birth. In her mind, there was nothing more meaningful than pouring herself into her family. In my mind, there was no one better for our child to be influenced and taught by. As perfect of a wife that she was, I knew she would be an even more amazing mother.

As the months flew by, we made all the preparations to welcome our new bundle of love. I completed and passed my paramedic course load and earned my paramedic license. Everything was falling right into place.

As we approached the delivery date, I scheduled some time off work to spend at home with Leigh-Ann and our expected daughter, Hannah. When I returned to work, I would be promoted to paramedic along with a much needed and significant raise in pay.

I spent three weeks at home soaking up every ounce of my new daughter. Every little thing she did pulled strings in my heart. I watched my wife in amazement as she assumed the role of a mother seamlessly.

Looking back, I feel like we were both naturals, even though we had no idea what we were doing. We poured ourselves into Hannah and each other. The sleepless nights brought us closer together as husband and wife. It was going to tear me apart to return to work, but I knew that I was now the sole breadwinner in the house. My wife and I decided that she would stay at home, even if it was a struggle, and I would pick up enough overtime to carry us financially.

All too soon the day came for me to return to work. I woke up and prepared for my shift. My wife was up feeding Hannah and kissed me goodbye.

After arriving at work, I walked into our headquarters and noticed a weird tension. I asked one of my colleagues what was going on. He told me that there has been talk of selling the company and a lot of people were panicking. I shook it off and prepared for my shift.

After about two weeks of my standard shifts, I was back in full stride. Then, on one of my regular overtime shifts, I was called into headquarters. I figured that I would be getting my promotion and assuming my new duties soon.

I walked into our director's office and took a seat. I could tell by his tone that something was off. He started the conversation by apologizing then led into the struggles that the company had been having and the number of people who were being affected. I started to zone out, and I knew where this was leading. The rumors were right: the company was sinking.

He tried to comfort me by complimenting my work ethic and my ability to be led. After the pleasantries, he told me that they had to let me go. Punching me in the gut would have been received better. I protested and told him that I would stay at the EMT level if that meant keeping my job. He wasn't even able to look me in the eye, and he responded by apologizing one last time and then motioned to the door. Calmly, I walked out of his office and collected my things.

As I sat in my vehicle, I could feel the entire world crashing down on me. I began to cry and kept a steady stream of tears the entire ride home. I tried to think of a benign way to tell Leigh-Ann that now we were both unemployed with a newborn, without sending her into a panic attack.

I walked through our front door to a surprised wife. She

could tell by the look in my eyes that something was majorly wrong. I broke down and explained that I had just been laid off. Without skipping a beat, she walked over, wrapped her arms around me and said, "It's going to be okay," with a calm and confident voice.

READER RESCUE – From early on in our relationship, Leigh-Ann and I were very much in love. We always had support from her parents up until the moment I asked to propose. I felt like they looked at me like a son. It's funny though how deep-down people can hide their true feelings.

Since then, both sets of parents have wanted to be part of our lives. We do have an ongoing relationship, but there is definitely a sense of emotional walls and distance. I think those walls will be around until all the emotions are talked through thoroughly.

Leigh-Ann has made multiple attempts to talk it out and tell her mom how she feels. The last and final time she tried to bring it up, she was met with, "Leigh-Ann, when are you going to move past this?"

Her father came right out and said he did not want to talk about it when he was reacclimating to our lives after turning his back on us for years.

Hopefully, one day they'll allow us to sit down and get our emotions out on the table. In order to gain closure, it would be beneficial to express how their actions affected us and then find a way to overcome that hurt. Never talking about it and pushing it away like it never happened can lead to harboring ill feelings and create awkwardness.

Chapter Four

Part 1

Back to the Basics

"It's humbling to start fresh. It takes a lot of courage. But it can
be reinvigorating. You just have to put your ego
on a shelf and tell it to be quiet."
- Jennifer Ritchie Payette

The proceeding months proved extremely difficult for us
financially. We struggled to keep our noses above water and
clung to the hope of receiving a job offer soon. I applied to
dozens of jobs, both as a paramedic and in unrelated fields. I
would have accepted any offer that would have helped provide
for my wife and daughter.

After no call backs or potential prospects, I started to panic
inside. I could feel the weight of the world crushing me, and all
I could do was watch as my wife worried more and more every
day, especially as we blew through our small savings trying to
make it day-to-day. I was completely defeated and embarrassed
by the situation, and even though Leigh-Ann was standing by
my side unhesitatingly, I was ashamed to look her in the face.

I found my comfort in food, which only increased my
anxiety even more. I was seemingly broken. I no longer held

my head high and soon resembled that overweight, timid, anxious and deflated child that I had suppressed for so many years.

After two months of blindly sinking, I finally received the phone call we were so desperately needing. It was from a district chief from a Florida County EMS provider, asking me to come in for an interview.

Not only was this my dream job, but they were wanting to conduct the interview the following week. I graciously accepted the interview and ran to the living room to tell Leigh-Ann the good news. I was met with a sigh of relief and tears of joy. We were so happy to have the prospect of a job in the emergency medical field. With this flood of emotion, we didn't even stop to think about the fact that if I received the offer and accepted the position, we would have to move approximately four hours away from all of our friends and family. We would be moving away from everything we ever knew and were familiar with. Looking at Hannah sleeping peacefully in her bassinet, it didn't matter. We would both move to the edge of the world if it meant providing a good life for her.

I was bursting at the seams with happiness in anticipation of the upcoming interview. I scurried to my closet and pulled out my one and only dress shirt and slacks.

I slid the shirt on and pulled up the pants. I was disgusted by my findings: neither the shirt nor the slacks were even close to fitting.

My first thought was, *these must be Leigh-Ann's former work slacks.* I quickly discovered that these were in fact my dress pants, and this was in fact my waistline. I looked at Leigh-Ann and laughed. I was still enjoying the afterglow of the great news I had received minutes earlier. I told her that we needed to run up to the store to get me an outfit for my upcoming interview, and she agreed.

We jumped in the car and headed to the only store we could afford at the time, Walmart. I quickly made my way to the men's clothing section and gathered a bunch of items to try on.

Everything I grabbed was too small for my ever-expanding circumference. I was typically a size thirty-six. So, I loaded up on a few thirty-eights and forties but had no luck. I then tried on a pair of forty-twos, still to no avail. I asked Leigh-Ann to grab me a pair of forty-fours, because I was too embarrassed to even exit the dressing room. She repeated my request to confirm that she had heard me right.

"Forty-fours?" she asked in the form of a question.

I confirmed in a monotone voice, and she could tell I didn't want to discuss it. She came back a few moments later with the slacks. I slid them on, and to my dismay, they fit like Cinderella's glass slipper.

As I stood there in the closet-sized dressing room, I stared at the smudged mirror, and I couldn't help but ask myself, *what happened, and how did I let myself slip this far?* After changing back to my clothes and gathering up my emotions, I exited the dressing room and headed towards the register with size forty-four pants and an XL dress shirt in hand.

When we arrived home, I made my way to the bathroom. Once again, I found myself sitting on that porcelain throne of shame, staring at myself in the mirror.

I finally worked up the courage to remove our scale from the closet, dust it off and strip down. Now was the moment of truth. I knew that I had steadily gained weight since starting EMT school, but I had no idea how much. I knew the only clothes that fit me were athletic shorts with an elastic waist and

63

an ill-fitting pair of "relaxed" jeans. I exhaled every ounce of breath from my lungs, for I wanted to be as light as possible. The digital display of the scale blinked back and forth as it measured my weight, and my heart seemed to mimic the same cadence. I was not prepared for the digital jury to come to a verdict of two hundred and ninety-seven pounds.

I stepped off the scale and allowed it to rest. I stepped on it again, this time in protest: there was no way I was two hundred and ninety-seven pounds! The last number I remember seeing was two hundred and five, when I entered EMT school two years earlier.

I stepped off the scale and attempted to swallow its findings. I was completely devastated. I was so ashamed of myself, not because of the weight, but because I had no idea how far I had slipped. I had completely stopped monitoring myself, and my physical, mental and emotional wellbeing was suffering.

I pulled myself together before exiting the bathroom and went back to trying to distract myself with the joy of having a job interview in a couple of days.

Finally, the morning of my job interview arrived, and I woke up at the crack of dawn to get ready. The interview was approximately four hours from my home, and I wanted to arrive early. I thought about how I would answer my interview questions during the entire drive. I focused on how I would come across and how I would answer any questions clearly and precisely. The drive that took four hours felt as if it were only thirty minutes.

As I sat in the waiting area, waiting to be called back for my interview, I sized up my competition.

After quickly scanning the room, I realized that I was

probably the most out-of-shape person sitting in it. Every other person who was there applying for *MY* position appeared fit and in shape.

As my name was called, I stood up and walked to the conference room with the captain who summoned me. Upon entering the interrogation chambers, I found myself eye-to-eye with four stone-faced command officers. They sat there in their pristinely pressed uniforms, arms crossed, sizing me up from my head to my toes.

I felt my heart rate increase, and I thought about Leigh-Ann and Hannah, who were counting on me to perform at my absolute best during this interview. I decided right then that it didn't matter that I was easily eighty pounds heavier than the next heaviest person in the room, and I would make them see the confidence that I had.

I stood up straight, approached each interviewer with purpose, firmly shook hands with each while maintaining eye contact, and then I took my seat and sat up as stiff as a board. I answered each question to the best of my ability while projecting as much confidence as possible.

After my interview, one of the commanding officers walked me to the exit. He told me it was a pleasure meeting me and they would be making their decisions within two to three weeks, but he looked forward to working with me.

I felt about one hundred pounds lighter as I walked to my car. I immediately called Leigh-Ann and told her that the interview had gone great and I was confident I would be offered a position. After we took a minute to take a deep breath and breathe a sigh of relief, we discussed the interview more in depth. I told her that I absolutely hated being the most unfit person in a room, and I planned on making some radical changes when I got home. Keeping in her nature, I was met with nothing but support and belief that I could do anything I set my mind to.

I arrived home and started throwing out all the junk food in the house. I threw away unopened containers of ice cream, cookies, chips and snack crackers. I emptied two-liter containers of Coke and Cherry Coke down the sink drain. As I purged all the unhealthy foods in our kitchen, I felt a strange feeling of empowerment that I hadn't felt since being let go from my previous job.

I felt like I was on the verge of getting my life back. I told my wife exactly how much I weighed and what I wanted to get down to. I told her that I was planning on making healthy foods and exercise part of my daily life. She was ecstatic to see my zest and me deciding to take charge of my life. I had wallowed in my own self-pity long enough. *NOW, IT WAS TIME FOR A CHANGE.*

After a week of healthy eating and nightly walks around my neighborhood, I started seeing positive results, mostly to my mental health. I started feeling better about myself almost immediately. Everything started to trend in the right direction.

One afternoon, Leigh-Ann, Hannah and I were out on a walk when my phone rang. I didn't know the number, but I recognized the area code. It was the outcome of my interview! I glanced at Leigh-Ann in excitement before answering. She mirrored the excitement and tried to listen intently. After exchanging pleasantries, the deputy chief on the other end of the phone cut right to the point: he extended a job offer to me. I failed miserably at trying to play it cool and answered with what could best be described as a squeal.

"YES! Thank you, you won't be disappointed."

After giving me all the details of their hiring process and timelines, he thanked me for my interview and said he looked forward to working with me. THREE months; I had three months to transform myself back into a man I was proud of. I was pumped for a job opportunity, but I also wanted to make sure that I was not the most out-of-shape guy in the department.

Part 2

Spark

I was a man on fire! I decided that when it came time to start my new job, I would be a completely different man. I did not want to be the most out-of-shape and unhealthy crew member on the rescue. I wanted to be as sure in my physical capabilities as I was in my knowledge and skill set. I made the choice to better my life, and the only activity I had ever known to have a proven history of benefits was running. I decided to dig through our closet, pull out an old, worn-out pair of running shoes and lace up.

As I stepped out of the door, I breathed in the humid, muggy and heat-soaked air that Florida in springtime was known for. I knew it had been some time since my last run, so I was planning on taking it nice and easy.

I decided to just run an "easy" mile, and then I would slowly build on that week by week. After all, I didn't want to go out too hard and burn myself out. I walked to the end of our driveway to warm my legs up before I started a nice, slow trot on the roadway.

It was only a matter of seconds, literally SECONDS, before my body and brain screamed, *"WHAT THE HELL ARE WE DOING?"*

I tried to calm my mind, but my brain did not contain enough oxygen to comprehend the positive self-talk.

My chest burned with every labored and desperate gasp of the humid, sticky air. My brain screamed at me to stop; it convinced me that death was imminent if I continued down this reckless path of self-improvement.

I tried to ignore the panicked begging from my brain, but within seconds my body joined in on the mutiny. My legs began to shake and feel unsteady, my back began to lock up and spasm and my lungs felt as if they were shanking my heart with some makeshift jailhouse shiv.

I tried to suck in as much air as I could through my bone-dry mouth, but my throat felt as if it were closing up.

It was at this moment that I knew, I had screwed up!

I quickly made the executive decision to abort this attempt of death by jog. I came to a stop, bent over, put my hands on my knees and tried not to pass out as I gasped for air.

The floating stars that were appearing before me distracted me from the fact that my heart rate matched that of a person on meth wrestling a grizzly. My knees shook and the road began to spin. I sat down on the curb and tried to bring my body out of survival mode.

As my breathing became more and more effective, my body and mind began to stabilize. With shaky legs I stood up, and started to slowly walk to my starting point, which was only about one hundred yards away.

As I retreated back home, I was overtaken by disappointment. I couldn't believe how out of shape I had become. I knew I was going to be a little slower, but I didn't anticipate the entire train coming off the tracks.

After arriving home, there I stood in the-all-too-familiar position of looking at myself in the mirror with disgust. I found myself once again drowning in self-loathing and self-pity. At this point I knew my journey to reclaim my self-esteem was just now beginning.

After I decided that I was not going to give up on the day, I headed back outside and decided to take it A LOT slower. I checked my surroundings to make sure there were no onlookers and I headed off again. I decided that I would just run to my neighbor's mailbox, a finish line that was roughly fifteen yards away. I engaged in a slow trot and focused my entire mind on my breathing and my next step.

I made it to the mailbox while maintaining my upright position. I was completely winded and gasping for air, but I was still upright. After crossing the mailbox, I decided to switch to walking. I walked at a brisk pace while struggling to catch my breath.

Once I felt adequately oxygenated, I zeroed in on the next mailbox and switched back to my "run" pace. I made it again, and I came to the realization that even though this pattern may be uncomfortable, it was sustainable for my current fitness level.

I continued this pattern of attack for a full two miles. This made a complete circle around my neighborhood. Once I arrived back home, I felt a multitude of feelings, both good and bad. I felt ashamed that this type of tempo was what I was reduced to. I felt embarrassed that someone my age was unable to even run one "simple" mile.

However, under the shame and embarrassment, I felt a small sense of accomplishment: after all, I didn't give up. I decided I would focus on this small spark of pride.

I made a pact with myself that I would repeat this workout every day until I was able to build on it. I kept my fingers crossed that if I focused on fanning this small spark, I could build enough momentum to start a raging fire.

Part 3

Inferno

I kept my promise to myself and repeated my circle-of-shame workout every day for weeks to come. I gave one hundred percent focus to healthy living, including my diet decisions. I stuck to a very rigid diet of lean proteins with loads of vegetables and fruits and only water to drink. I learned that when fueled properly, I felt better both physically and mentally... I know, I know... ground-breaking, right?

I also learned that in the absence of junk food, my body would actually CRAVE healthy alternatives. I started to find joy in fresh fruits and wholegrain snacks. My brain looked forward to grilled fish and chicken in the same way it used to look forward to fast food and desserts.

Having the proper amount of nutrition made all the difference in the world. I noticed that my depression started to subside, and my anxiety levels dropped significantly.

I started to take pride in myself and appreciate the man in the mirror once again. I would weigh myself on a weekly basis and celebrate the gains, or should I say "loss" of the week past.

The slacks that once fit like Cinderella's slippers were now hanging off my hips. I was able to place both arms into the buttoned waistline with room to spare. However, I did make a declaration that I would not let a number on the scale dictate the way I looked at myself, because after all, I was feeling tons better.

While I wasn't basing my happiness on the findings of the scale, I would be a liar if I said that seeing the number drop didn't excite me and fan my flames. After the first two months, I was down almost fifty pounds. What I lost in weight, I tripled in self-esteem.

I slowly added distance and intensity to my running workouts during this time. I found that the more and more weight I lost the easier running had become... again... I know, ground-breaking.

I found myself running for longer and longer without the need to stop and suck air like my life depended on it. I would run five to six mailboxes with a much higher intensity without a walk break. At the time, I thought running meant always putting forth a ninety to one hundred percent effort every time I wasn't walking. I was basically running sprints between walk breaks.

One crazy day, I decided to see how far I could run without taking a walk break. I knew I would need to slow my pace WAY down and focus on my breathing as if I were instructing a Lamaze class.

I laced up my shoes and grabbed a final swig of water before toeing the imaginary starting line in front of my mailbox. I took my usual glance at my surroundings and confirmed no one was watching me.

Then I set off. I focused my full attention on my stride and breathing. I fought every instinct and urge to run as fast as I had on my past runs. I maintained a slower but strong cadence. I felt as if I were just cruising. My breathing was deep and unlabored; I couldn't feel my pulse bounding in my throat like I was used to. I was comfortably uncomfortable at my pace. My brain screamed, "You're going way too slow; you're not doing anything!"

I redirected my attention to my body and the feedback I was receiving from it. My body seemed to say, "If you just continue at this pace, I won't let you down."

I decided to continue my pace and ignore my judgmental brain. After all, I wasn't there to set any land speed records; I just wanted to see how far I could go.

As I approached the quarter-mile marker, I realized that this was the farthest I had run in years.

My brain protested in anticipation of exhaustion and pain. I should have been completely exhausted by this point, but I seemed comfortable. My body continued to reassure me at my current pace. I sailed past the light post that marked the half-mile point. I felt invigorated: passing that pole without stopping or passing out was a huge feat for me!

I celebrated by singing out loud while I ran. Eminem's "Lose Yourself" was the song I had on repeat on my iPod; it just seemed so fitting. I completely lost myself in the run. I learned that once I stopped focusing on my brain's whining, it had no choice but to shut up.

Approaching the one-mile marker, I felt a rush of relief. I was back up to my personal best distance of one full mile without stopping, a distance I had not run since high school.

As I backed off my pace to bring the run to a stop, my body and brain harmoniously yelled, keep going! I hesitated for a second but then recovered my pace. I sailed by the one-mile marker, completely enamored with myself. I flirted with the idea of attempting two full miles. I completed a quick mental checklist of how my body was responding to the distance and pressed on.

As I continued to strategically place one foot in front of the other with purpose, I felt all the shame I had recently been living with stripped away. This was the first time in my life I was running for pure joy. Every other time I ran was to strictly meet distance, time or weight loss goals. This time was different: this time I was running because I wanted to. Because I could.

As my feet struck the ground, they created a rhythmic symphony of pride. I couldn't believe it; I was proud of myself again! Even though my weight was nowhere near what I wanted, I was proud of myself for taking charge of my life and changing it. I was proud because I was able to find some joy in my running. I was determined to keep chasing this sense of accomplishment.

I decided that I would no longer sprint between mailboxes like a maniac running from a swarm of hornets. I would focus more on the joy that I was experiencing in the moment. I would shift my focus from weight loss and punishment to enjoyment. I wanted to keep this feeling of happiness and incorporate it into my daily life.

As moving day approached, I was excited about the prospect of restarting my life with a clean slate and a passion for exercising. I was curious to see how deep this rabbit hole went.

We packed up our entire life into brown cardboard boxes. I was thankful that I was not packing the size forty-four pants! The feeling of emptiness that filled that waistline would be left behind in a now empty house.

I was ready to keep putting one foot in front of the other in all aspects of my life, and what started off as a small spark of hope was now a raging wildfire providing light to my future.

Reader Rescue – As disheartening as it is to have to start from square one, the old proverb says it best: a journey of a thousand miles really does start with a single step. Starting a new exercise regimen and taking charge of your life is hard enough on its own. The best advice that I can give is to walk your own path. Figure out what works best for you and set your own goals. Exercise, especially running, is hard enough on its own, let alone comparing yourself to others.

Chapter Five

Part 1

Highway To Hell

"It's all fun and games until somebody dies."
- Tom Hobbs

Life was good. As a matter of fact, life was great! It had been three months since our move, and life was finally seeming to stabilize. I was completely done with my training, and I was released by my field training officer to operate as a paramedic on my own.

I was slipping into my groove, formulating treatment strategies and gaining confidence to face whatever the public chose to throw at me. I studied my protocols, standing orders and guidelines frontwards and back. I committed them to memory and mentally placed myself in situations to prepare to use them with self-assurance. I loved my job and I loved being the person people called when they needed help.

I was still working out and running on a very consistent basis. I continued to shrink my waistline down while building my strength and endurance. I wanted to be sure that if I ever needed to carry a person down multiple flights of stairs that my body would be prepared and dependable.

I stuck to the promise I made myself and chased the joy of working out. I viewed it as a privilege to be able to freely move my body; after all, there was a ton of people who would trade anything to be able to lace up and go out for a run on a warm summer day.

I was so thankful for where we were in life. I felt privileged to be able to put my uniform on in the morning and place myself in the position to be the person someone called on in their time of need.

Aside from the personal pride I took in my individual job responsibilities, I worked with an incredible crew of people. My partner, Erik, and I were both paramedics and new to the county. We were hired in the same hiring class and completed training together. We acclimated to each other's treatment style quickly and could almost predict what the other needed before we had a chance to ask for it.

Erik was a former US Marine, a family man and an all-round great guy. He was really dialed in and fixated on his fitness as well. He never knew it, but he was a huge role model for me regarding my running. He was lean, laser focused and fast. I used to make jokes that his stride was somewhere between a gazelle and mongoose. Erik made running look effortless, and I hoped to someday be at that point. Furthermore, he was a quiet and collected guy and didn't like to talk about himself much, but during the times I could get him to talk about running, I hung on everything he said.

He told me how he ran the Jacksonville Marathon, and I was dumbfounded. I knew a marathon was far, but I had no idea that it was 26.2 miles! I would sit and ponder, how could someone run that far in one effort? It seemed almost superhuman. I was broken after two miles. I was happy and proud, but broken, nonetheless.

Erik would give me tips about running as we sat around waiting for an emergency to be dispatched. He described his ideal pace, stride, foot landing, form, nutrition and almost every other aspect and trait that breeds a successful long-distance runner. He discussed many mistakes new runners make when they first start off and encouraged me to sign up for my first 5k. Erik further motivated me by saying, "If you can run two miles during training, you can complete a 5k."

I quickly agreed with a bolstered attitude and instantly decided to sign up for my first 5k. If Erik thought I could handle it, who was I to disagree? The only issue I faced was the fact that I had no idea what a 5k was.

I quickly jumped onto Google and searched the question, *how far is a 5k?* The wizards at Google quickly provided me with my answer: 3.1 miles.

After finding out that a 5k was over a full mile farther than I had ever run, I would be a liar if I said I wasn't intimidated. I second-guessed myself and my abilities, but hey, if a "real" runner believed I could do it, then I had better give it a try.

I looked up the local running club schedule and found a 5k that was about one month out. I decided that this would give me plenty of time to train and build up my endurance a bit more.

For an entire month, I focused every spare thought on my upcoming race. I completely engrossed myself in running culture. I spent most of my free time researching running articles and consuming a gratuitous amount of running-related YouTube videos. I even bought every running magazine I could find on the shelves of my local bookstores.

I was driven to perform my very best. I mean, after all, this would be my initiation to becoming a "real" runner. I visualized crossing the finish line during every single training run. I daydreamed about being able to consider myself a "real" runner and nonchalantly working the fact that I had run a 5k into everyday conversation. I was a locomotive aimed at crossing that finish line. Nothing would stop me!

As race day approached, I made sure to hydrate and stretch every night leading up to race morning. The night before, I laid out the clothes and shoes that I planned on wearing. I woke up super early to make sure I had plenty of time to arrive at the starting line and early enough to pick up my race bib and swag bag.

After arriving at the starting line, I felt completely overwhelmed. There were a couple of hundred people there to run this race.

I stood in line at the bib table to pick up my first ever race bib. The lady on the other side of the table handed me a paper bib with three safety pins held together by a fourth. I took the items from the volunteer with the confidence that suggested I'd done this before. As I exited the line, bib in hand, I anxiously fumbled around with the safety pins and bib until I figured out how and where to secure it to my shirt.

I must have readjusted that numbered piece of paper eleven to twelve times until I got it perfectly straight.

I looked around at the sea of people and tried to find a place among the crowd, a place where I would blend in while being surrounded by people of the same fitness caliber.

Everywhere I looked there seemed to be people who appeared to belong there, athletic and confident people, whose performance would surely blow me out of the water. I briefly thought to myself, *this is a huge mistake and I don't belong here.* As I was starting to develop an exit strategy back to my car, a voice came over the PA system and announced, "All runners, please head to the starting line. This is the one-minute warning."

I instinctively moved with the flow of the pack, and within seconds I found myself standing mid-pack, awaiting the final countdown before the gun went off. I could feel my heart pounding in my chest while I listened to the music they had playing over the loudspeakers. A barrage of thoughts raced through my head.

What happens if I can't keep up?

What happens if I have to take a walk break?

What happens if I have to drop out of the race?

What happens if I can't finish?

By the time my mind could process all the things that could go wrong, the announcer started his countdown from, "Ten…"

My heart raced as I thought, *what am I doing?*

"Nine…"

I don't belong here!

"Eight…"

Why did I decide to do this?

"Seven…"

Is it too late to leave the corral?

"Six…"

I need to get out of here!

"Five…"

There's no way of backing out now.

"Four…"

Might as well try to enjoy it.

"Three…"

Just put one foot in front of the other!

"Two…"

Holy shit, you forgot to breathe; take a breath, you idiot!

"One…"

Here we go!

The starting pistol's bang cut through the noisy air as if Thor himself had pulled the trigger. I gathered myself and quieted my mind as the crowded corral started slowly moving forward, one baby step at a time.

I slowly adjusted to the fact that I was stuck. I was being swept downstream like a lifeless log stuck in the white-water current of forward progression.

We continued forward like cattle being forced through a funnel point. Soon enough, myself and the people around me reached the point of the start line, where everyone was starting up their running stride.

I slowly increased my pace until it mirrored the speed I was used to during my training runs. My senses were completely overloaded. Between the cheering crowd, the music blasting over the loudspeakers and the intimidating shaking of cowbells, I was one hundred percent distracted from my nerves.

After clearing the starting area, the runners started to thin out a bit. We all fell into a smooth, comfortable pace while following our own personal invisible lane. I took a quick look around and noticed the determination and drive on everyone's faces around me. My mind, which was cluttered with a thousand negative thoughts just moments earlier, was now overflowing with positivity.

I am actually doing it!

I am running a race!

Am I now an actual runner?

Does this put me in the same category as Erik?
Is it really this simple?

My heart raced, not because of a reckless pace or anxiety but because I felt like I belonged here.

As I passed the marker for mile two, I started to feel the side effects of this distance, and the excitement and adrenaline started to burn off. It was very apparent in my brain that every step I took was a new step in foreign territory. My brain started to panic with the prospect of having another whole mile left.

I remembered my training runs, when my brain would try to hijack my drive and discourage me into quitting. I remembered how ashamed of myself I felt when I quit because I was uncomfortable. I made a declaration that I was going to finish this race as if my life depended on it. I dug in deep and maintained pace. I focused every oxygenated brain cell on my breathing and stride. I continued to place one foot in front of the other and maintain determination.

As I approached the final turn of the course, I could hear the celebratory commotion of the finish line. I ran past small groups of onlookers, who all took the time to send cheers my way.

They yelled, "COME ON, RUNNER, KEEP IT UP. YOU'RE ALMOST THERE!"

I looked up, smiled and gave them an appreciative nod. I refocused my eyes to the course, and I could now see the finish line! It was one of the most beautiful sights I've ever seen. I threw caution to the wind and started sprinting. I passed multiple people as I gave it my all, leaving everything I had on the course.

As I crossed the finish line and walked down the finishers' chute, I soaked it all in and made sure that moment was burned into my mind.

A volunteer handed me a small paper cup of watered down Powerade and a half of a banana. Although it seemed like a small finisher token, that banana and Powerade may as well have been manna from heaven. I downed the drink with one gulp and basically inhaled the banana.

I made my way over to the finishers' area, where positive affirmations and high fives were in abundance.

Life Rule one hundred and thirty-five: never pass up a high five.

I was taken back by all the support that was given by the other runners both during and after the race. From the moment I started running the race to standing around the finishers' area, I was bombarded by, "Great job", "looking strong" and "Way to go!"

This was completely different to what I had expected. I never thought that people who were all in competition with one another could be so supportive of everyone else's personal achievement and success.

Maybe there was more to races than the racing… Maybe there was more to running than just running. Either way, I was hooked. I couldn't wait to tell everyone about my weekend endeavor. I was swelling with pride, and there was nothing that could rob this joy from me.

Part 2

Detour

The next morning, I arrived at HQ and started completing inventory on our truck for the upcoming shift. I was waiting for Erik to arrive so I could brag my way through a play-by-play of the 5k and receive my knighting into the exclusive "real runners" club.

I was still basking in the afterglow of my success from the day before when Erik arrived. Every muscle in my body was stiff and sore, but my pride couldn't flex harder.

As he approached, he could tell by my limp that I had a war story to exchange. After letting him know the truck was ready to go, we logged in and made ourselves available for service. We completed all the morning chores before I attempted to tell him about the race. I wanted his full, undivided attention.

Just as I started to tell him about the pre-race jitters I had battled, the emergency tones dropped... of course!

"Medic 35, Medic 35... Code 3 for a motor vehicle accident," dispatch announced over our radios.

I looked at Erik and said, "To be continued," as my story was interrupted.

Once dispatch provided us with the location of the call, we started rolling. We listened to the radio intently, because this particular accident seemed to be significant based on the number of units that were being dispatched. After the dispatcher had the cavalry mobilized, she provided us a with second-hand witness synopsis.

"Medic 35, you are en route to a motor vehicle accident. Reports describe a mid-size sedan versus a dump truck, head-on collision. Significant damage, entrapment and airbag deployment noted."

As we neared the scene, we could tell that this was going to be a major accident based on the traffic standstill. We engaged the shoulder of the road and made our way to the front of the gridlock.

After clearing the traffic, we realized that this wreck was indeed extreme. We were looking at a mid-size sedan accordioned into the front of a dump truck. The impact had crushed the car and placed the engine nearly in the back seat and trunk. I immediately picked up the radio and requested air support, but unfortunately my request was denied due to inclement weather.

The fire engine was already on scene starting the extraction of the two occupants in the sedan. In the driver's seat there was a middle-aged woman, pinned by the steering wheel and half of the front end. In the passenger seat was her husband, pinned to his seat by unidentifiable engine components. The entire length of the car was reduced to about four to five feet. The couple seemed to be sitting in the front and back seats at the same time.

Just as the sky opened up and started to pour on us, the second transport crew arrived and started working on their patient, the male passenger. I was busy working on the driver and didn't see what type of specific injuries he had suffered. All I knew was that there was obvious closed head trauma and multiple open long bone fractures. He was unresponsive during the entire extraction, roughly fifteen to twenty minutes.

My patient, the driver, was screaming the entire time. Every attempt we made to calm her was completely and understandably ineffective. As we dug through the wreckage, I started getting a much clearer idea of the mess we were going to have once she was freed.

She had multiple fractures in both arms from clinging to the steering wheel during impact. We noted major facial trauma and deep lacerations to her cheeks and forehead from the shrapnel that was flung from under the hood into the passenger compartment.

We were unable to assess from her abdomen down because of the wreckage sitting on her lap. She kept screaming, "MY LEGS, I CAN'T FEEL MY LEGS!"

I knew once we pulled the front end of this vehicle off her lap, things were going to go south quickly. Whenever someone is pinned for an extended period of time, there's usually an abrupt and significant drop in blood pressure once they are released.

We placed a cervical collar on her to protect her from any further spinal injuries. I started a large bore IV in her left jugular vein and started pumping fluid in as quickly as possible to offset any drop in blood pressure. Once the fire engine crew pulled the engine debris off her lap, we were privy to the carnage underneath.

We rotated her out of the steel coffin which was once a family vehicle and onto a long backboard. We secured her down and loaded her up into the back of the ambulance. She continued, "OH GOD, I CAN'T FEEL MY LEGS," through visceral, blood-curdling screams.

I looked down at her legs and both were completely

mangled and hanging on by thin threads of flesh. Her calves looked like they had been run over by a freight train, both completely flattened and flayed open. Both feet were completely deformed and indistinguishable as human feet. From the waist down she looked like someone who had stepped on a landmine.

We continued to maintain a strong blood pressure and were able to provide her with a small dose of morphine. During mass trauma calls, it's a very strong empathetic instinct to help the patient get out of pain by any means necessary.

The issue with this is that morphine and other pain medications can have a pretty strong negative impact on blood pressure. Fortunately, in this case we were able to maintain a strong blood pressure and mental status.

The morphine had a positive but minimal effect on the pain. It did reduce her instinctual pleas for help but also calmed her down just enough to remind her that her husband was also in the car. Once her husband entered the front of her mind, she started screaming once again. At this point she was utterly inconsolable.

The transport to the local trauma center seemed to take forever; in retrospect, it only took roughly fifteen minutes. After arriving, we unloaded and passed off care to the well-capable trauma team. They started their assessment and prepped her for surgery. The surgeon told his team that she was going to lose both of her legs just above the knee.

Now that our duty was complete, Erik and I collected our gear and headed back out to our truck. On our way out, I overheard two nurses say that her husband had passed away roughly ten to fifteen minutes before we had arrived. I acted like I hadn't heard what they were talking about and kept walking to the ambulance bay. I was already emotionally exhausted, and this was just the FIRST call of the day.

Once we had cleared the call, restocked and made our unit available again, we found ourselves sitting idly at the fire station. We didn't even get out of the truck; we just sat there, reflecting on the events that had just transpired. Erik broke the silence.

"So, you were telling me about your race yesterday…"

I looked at him and replied flatly, "It was good," and that was the end of the conversation.

At that point, completing a 5k no longer seemed like a big deal. How could I bring myself to brag about running a race while this poor lady was having her legs removed as we spoke? Not only was she going to wake without her legs, she was also going to find out that she was now a widow. It didn't seem fair or right to caress my pride in completing a 5k when there was someone literally struggling to stay alive.

For the most part, my next few shifts were pretty unmemorable. However, I did find myself dwelling on the driver, who lost so much. I found myself replaying the scene and events of the transport over and over in my head during my quiet times.

The problem was that my running time was my quiet time. Every step I ran I felt as if I were taunting her. She invaded my mind and set up camp. There was no avoiding her. I reduced my running a great deal, because I was hopeful that I would move on soon; after all, I'd seen other terrible things that didn't have this type of impact on me. My logic suggested that if I thought about her when I ran, if I stopped running, I'd stop thinking of her. For the next few months, I barely ran at all and kept my mind distracted with work. I started picking up overtime shifts almost every day I was off.

It was working. As long as I kept myself focusing on my next patient, my brain didn't have time to dwell on past patients. The relief I once found in running was replaced with an unexplainable and relentless drive to work as many hours as possible. I set my cruise control on full throttle and gave little to no regard to the things that were proven to help my mental and emotional health, largely my running.

I learned an important lesson: the main problem with missing runs is that if you do it enough, soon you won't miss running at all.

Part 3

Redline

Neil Young once said, "It's better to burn out than fade away." In retrospect, this seemed to be my mantra pertaining to my life. During the following years, I was a machine. I completely submerged myself in my job. I was working a ridiculous number of hours, and the only running I was doing was running myself ragged. Working seemed to be my safety net. The busier I stayed, the less time I had to think about all the death and trauma.

However, I would be disingenuous if I implied that I didn't get addicted to the pride that came with being known as the "dependable one" within my company and with the money I was raking in. I was working an average of one hundred and sixty to one hundred and seventy hours every TWO weeks. Some pay periods would reflect two hundred plus hours. I had a great reputation with my command staff as one of the truest employees, who never complained about extra hours. At home, I was able to finally provide the finances and experiences that my wife and daughter deserved. The only issue was that I couldn't be home to take part in those experiences.

Finances and reputation were great, but my main reward was the distraction that work provided from myself. I was terrified to be alone with my own thoughts. On one hand, having constant distraction was a blessing; on the other, it was adding new trauma, stress and exhaustion to the old camel's back. I didn't have an exit strategy; I was stuck in the perpetual paradox of masking past trauma with fresh trauma. I wasn't burning the proverbial candle at both ends, I was soaking it in kerosene and attacking it with a flamethrower.

I lived in a constant state of exhaustion. I felt that if I took a break to catch my breath, I would be overwhelmed by the thoughts of all the patients I was exposed to. During my entire career as a medic, I was considered a "black cloud". A "black cloud" is as pleasant as it sounds: it usually describes someone who typically loses the luck of the draw and ends up getting dispatched to the most extreme, screwed-up calls. For whatever reason, if there was a major accident, shooting, stabbing, cardiac arrest, pediatric issue or complicated respiratory call, it always seemed to land in my lap.

Despite my terrible luck with calls, I continued to whore myself to the overtime demands of my company. The constant needs and demands of a high-performance 911 system is a pimp that will continue taking and taking until there's nothing left. I would naively work six to seven days a week, putting in twelve- to twenty-four-hour days at a time. The rare days that I had off, I was completely useless, because I was understandably exhausted. I felt as if I were redlining a race car, with only fumes in the tank. I knew this lifestyle was not sustainable. My only question was, *what was going to go first, my physical ability to keep this up OR my mental capabilities?*

I missed my wife and my daughter greatly. When I was on shift, they were all I thought about when I wasn't running calls. I felt regretful that I wasn't home more, and I felt like I was missing out on watching Hannah develop as she grew like a weed. Leigh-Ann and I maintained a very close and loving marriage. She knew that I was working so much to make sure that we were comfortable and could afford to live in the good side of town and make sure Hannah had everything she needed.

What Leigh-Ann did not know was how much I was struggling to deal with the insane amount of death and trauma. She knew I had a difficult job but had no clue of the effects it was having on my emotional and mental well-being.

I became completely reclusive. My communication shut down and I did my best to hide behind a facade. I couldn't even understand why I was feeling the way I was, let alone explain it to someone else. Knowing something is wrong and watching yourself slowly slip away but having no idea where to even begin to detangle the emotional webs is a weird headspace to be in.

At home, I always felt like I was on edge. I noticed that I started having a shorter temper and would become disproportionately angry with little things. I started to hate going out in public, especially around large, loud crowds. I started to despise people.

Could you blame me?

I was typically a front-row witness to the potential for stupidity, violence and atrocities by humankind. After all, it takes a special kind of evil to murder a child or use a hot stove top as a disciplinary tool. Likewise, I didn't even want to explore the psychological rotting one must have to use their own stroke-victim mother as a sex slave. I have seen the capacity and depths of human depravedness, and it runs deep.

Usually at home I could pin my emotional instability on being tired. Even during times when I was able to spend the entire night in my own bed, I wasn't able to sleep. My mind was rushing one hundred miles a minute.

I was constantly seeing patients that I had witnessed die when I closed my eyes. I could hear kids crying and parents screaming as I lay my head down in my quiet bedroom. I remember one time Leigh-Ann had to wake me up because I was performing CPR chest compressions in the middle of our mattress.

I was completely burned out. Within my first few years in the service, I gained about ten years' worth of experience. It seemed like the only two things I did was work and complain about working.

I didn't have any hobbies, interests, or outlets. My running and exercising became a distant memory. I may have run one to two times a month, completing a few half-hearted miles each time. The only time I could motivate myself to lace up my running shoes was when I guilted myself into it. I no longer found joy in running. As a matter of fact, I no longer found joy in anything outside of being around my wife and daughter.

Although I didn't know it at the time, I was completely and utterly depressed. I felt dead inside.

I started to hate the person in the mirror YET AGAIN! I was slowly but surely packing the weight back on. Although it was nowhere near as much as it once was, it was enough to notice and feel.

I knew what I needed to do to feel better, I just couldn't bring myself to do it. I knew I needed to reduce my work hours and make time for healthy changes, like sleeping, eating right and exercising, to start with. I just couldn't find the motivation to. It's almost like I accepted the person I had become and felt like I didn't deserve any better.

On the surface I seemed fine. I kept a mask on, especially at work. The first responder field comes with a stigma that suggests that if you can't handle the stress, then you're not cut out for this field, and asking for help equates with weakness.

I didn't even admit that I needed to slow down to myself, let alone anyone else. I continued to keep my head down and press through with the hopes that one day everything would just magically fall into place for me.

I continued to force myself and bend the limits of my mental and physical endurance, all the while allowing my emotional well-being to slip further and further away from me.

Again, I knew what I needed to do but felt worthless and unworthy of happiness. I tried to take care of everyone who needed help, and the ones that I couldn't help took up permanent residence in my brain. I saw so much death and scarring of life that I felt like a complete failure inside.

I felt like a hypocrite, for I was supposed to help those people, and I couldn't even help myself. I was on a highway to hell with the pedal to the metal and zero regard for my own well-being. The problem with flying down this highway is that you will eventually reach its destination.

Reader Rescue – As I write these pages, it seems absolutely ludicrous that I used overtime to treat and deal with the ongoing stress and trauma. Unhealthy and ineffective coping skills are trademark traits of first responders, in my experience. A lot of us tend to deal with our problems by using avoidance and distraction. Working extra hours to distract from my issues at work was like crushing my left foot to distract from the pain of stubbing my right toe. Another insidious aspect of the downfall of one's mental health is isolation. Even though I was distracting myself and surrounding myself with people, my mental health caused me to feel completely alone.

Chapter Six

Part 1

Life in the Fast Lane

"I wish my head could forget what my eyes have seen."
- Dave Parnell

The mind is an extraordinary place. Its capabilities and potential are immeasurable. It has the capacity for love, sympathy, empathy, courage and humor, just to name a few. It has the prowess to navigate mathematics, philosophy, scientific theories, and the ability to detect the underlying tone behind passive-aggressive work emails.

With a single melody or note, the mind can recall every word to the first song you ever learned or take you right back to the first day of kindergarten with the single sniff of a new box of crayons.

Through a simple touch of a texture, it can surface memories of the scraping on a motorcycle helmet that housed a bodiless head or turn the laughter of children to a flashback of a child screaming while watching us try to save their mother, who was found dead in her bedroom after overdosing.

It's simply amazing how the mind can turn happiness into hell with a simple stimulation. I don't remember asking for the hell I've been through, and I most definitely didn't ask for the dismantling of my life, but along the way, in dealing with others' trauma and anguish, I ended up losing myself.

I still, and always will, remember my first major pediatric emergency. I can tell you everything about the scene down to how the air smelled that morning. It was a typical laidback Sunday. It was an overtime shift, so I wasn't working with Erik. The EMT I was working with was very new to the service and was still very green, a term that is synonymous with "rookie". We had just completed our truck check-in and had put ourselves in service. About two hours into waiting for a call, dispatch tones cut through the peaceful morning like an early detection air raid warning system.

"Medic 35, we need you Code 3 for an unresponsive pediatric."

Now, for the record, this type of call sounds unbelievably terrible, but we do run a ton of calls to "unresponsive pediatrics" who are just sleeping heavily and mom is having trouble waking them up fully. So, there was the potential for this to be another routine dry run, a 911 call that didn't require any treatment or transport.

As my partner and I entered the address into the GPS and started rolling towards the call, dispatch came back over the radio advising, "CPR in progress…"

At this point, we knew this WAS NOT going to be just another false alarm; this was going to be a matter of life and death.

As we arrived on scene, the fire engine was pulling up behind us, and I quickly prepped my mind to manage any scenario that I was about to walk into. After grabbing my jump bag full of gear, I briskly walked to the front door with the medic from the fire engine. As we approached the front door, we could hear screaming and cries.

"Hurry, hurry, we're in here... HELP, HELP, PLEASE!"

Just as I walked through the front door, a frantic father pushed a limp, lifeless baby body into my arms. The baby's mother was completely and understandably in panic mode. Her screams and cries penetrated my body and hijacked my adrenal system, which caused my body to dump every ounce of adrenaline into my bloodstream at once.

I looked down at the six-month-old baby in my arms and fought back my gasping reaction. He was a mixture of dark purple and blue from the neck up. He had a mouth full of vomit that was obstructing his airway. Holding a child's limp, lifeless body is the most unnatural thing a human can do.

I quickly retreated to my truck while performing chest compressions. After laying him on the stretcher, I told my partner to DRIVE! The medic and EMT from the fire engine jumped in the back with me to assist with treatment and off we went, flying down the fast lane, utilizing shoulders and medians to get to the hospital as quickly as possible.

I grabbed my tools to intubate while the EMT performed chest compressions and the other medic prepped the cardiac arrest medication. As I attempted to insert the breathing tube, I realized his airway was completely blocked by vomit. After digging and clearing the obstruction from the back of his throat, I was able to visualize his airway. I inserted the tube and quickly started providing him with much-needed concentrated oxygen. We gained intraosseous access, which is basically drilling into a bone to use as a route to push medications. Bone marrow access acts just as fast as a traditional IV and is a lot faster in a pinch.

After two to three rounds of highly oxygenated air and administration of advanced cardiac medications, we regained an organized heart rhythm on the cardiac monitor with a matching pulse.

WE DID IT... HE WAS BACK!

He was still unresponsive, but his heart was beating on its own. The three of us in the back of the truck all took a deep breath and gave a much-needed sigh of relief. I called the receiving hospital to put them on high alert and gave them an idea of what to expect in a few minutes.

We pulled into the hospital and quickly jumped out of the back door and unloaded the stretcher. As we walked through the EMS entrance, we were met by the receiving team of doctors, nurses and technicians. We handed over care and gave a full report. They quickly took over as we packed our gear up and left.

After cleaning the back of the truck and prepping for the next call, we took a brief moment to celebrate the outcome of such a grim situation. We shook each other's hands and complimented each other's performance while we tried to get our adrenaline back down to a manageable level. Complimenting each other's performance is the closest thing to "popping champagne" EMS workers do on shift.

After clearing that call, it was a few hours before I found myself back at the hospital, dropping off a routine patient. I swung by the room that we had dropped the baby off in. It was empty, clean and awaiting another patient. I figured that the baby boy had been moved upstairs to the pediatric ICU, but I decided to stop by the nurses' station to confirm. I asked the nurse how he was doing, and she looked at me and paused before saying, "I'm so sorry, he didn't make it."

Instantaneously, I felt as if someone had punched me in the gut. I clarified that I was asking about the six-month-old boy that we had brought in earlier in hopes that she was thinking about the wrong patient.

She confirmed, while fighting back tears, by saying, "After you guys left, he continued to go in and out of cardiac arrest until his little heart just wasn't strong enough."

I didn't know how to receive this information. I was devastated. I hung my head and walked back to my truck. My partner asked for a status update of the baby, and I just responded, "I don't know. He wasn't in the room, and his nurse was nowhere to be found. He must have been moved to PICU. I'm sure he's doing well."

I couldn't bring myself to share this burden. Even though I knew I had done everything I could, I couldn't help but question if there was more that I could have done. I finished off my twenty-four-hour shift completely devastated. I couldn't get that baby out of my head.

Everything about him was burned into my eyes and memory. I had no idea at the time, but this was a pivotal point in my life. It sent my mental health down the fast lane of anxiety and depression at breakneck speed. My mind started working overtime…

What if I wasn't a good paramedic?
What if I have another baby to work on?
What if I couldn't help?

I arrived home and greeted Leigh-Ann as usual. After kissing her good morning and changing out of my uniform, I went directly to the freezer. In it, I found a full bottle of Captain

Morgan rum. I pulled it out and poured a tall glass, only mixing it with ice. Leigh-Ann watched as I downed the entire glass. She recoiled and was taken back by my breakfast choice. I hadn't consumed that amount at that intensity ever in my life. She looked confused and asked, "Is everything okay? How was your shift?"

I replied, "Rough."

I didn't want to share what had happened, mainly because I had no words. She could see in my eyes that I had had a rough shift and didn't pry too much.

At this point in my life, I was a social drinker. I didn't really drink to get drunk, and to be completely honest, I didn't even like the taste of alcohol.

I sat on the couch staring blankly at whatever was on TV. Leigh-Ann was feeding Hannah and preparing for her day. I could feel the embrace of the alcohol slowly slip over me. The tension in my neck and shoulders slowly started easing and my mind, which was racing, started to slow down. I was no longer thinking of the baby or his parents; instead, I was just wanting to get some rest.

I kissed Leigh-Ann and Hannah on the cheek and said I was going to lay down for a couple hours. By the time my head hit the pillow, I was fully relaxed from my liquid relief.

I was worried that I wasn't going to be able to sleep off the thought of my day. Then I realized I had the answer to my speeding brain waiting for me in the freezer. It was a simple solution if I needed back up.

All of a sudden, I started to realize why it seemed like everyone in the first responder field seemed to drink more heavily than other people. It was the emergency brake to a speeding run-away mind.

Part 2

~~In Moderation~~
Immoderation

During the following months and into years, I continued to do what I did best: sink my heels into the ground and push forward. I never spoke to anyone about the impact that child had had on me, but I was thinking about him every day. He was typically the first thought I had in the morning and the last thought I had before drifting off to sleep. Looking back on it, I feel like my brain was using this child as a metaphor for ALL the trauma I was exposed to and not just this single patient.

I continued my kamikaze approach to dealing with trauma… work as much as possible to distract myself. I continued to slave away, picking up every available shift I could. I would call my supervisor and ask if they needed coverage anywhere in the city so that I didn't have to go home. My anxiety about being undistracted was significantly increasing day-by-day.

I missed home life terribly, and most of all I missed spending time with Leigh-Ann and Hannah. I missed the days where I could just sit and relax without my brain snowballing. I missed being myself and being able to be happy.

During my emotional downfall, it was almost like I forgot how to feel joy and happiness. I felt that I was a burden at home because I was always on edge and pointing out the negatives.

My baseline of anger and frustration always seemed to dictate the temperature of the house. If I was in a bad mood, then everyone was in a bad mood.

Leigh-Ann noticed the drastic change in my personality but chalked it up to being in a perpetual state of exhaustion. I was very convincing when I exclaimed that everything was fine, so convincing that I even began to believe the facade. She practically begged me to take time off, but I would completely disregard her advice because I was "the machine" and could handle anything.

My ego was in the driver's seat and driving my body into the ground, all because my mind didn't want to start the process of figuring out what was wrong with me. I was terrified of the reality.

At this stage, I was a few years into my career and completely burnt out. I was no longer the jovial person I once was. The passion to help others was replaced with the obligation to act during an emergency. I no longer looked at helping others as a privilege but started to see people in need as a burden. When we were dispatched to a call, I was annoyed. All I could think about was, *why are you bothering us* and *you better be dying.*

Now, before you start thinking that I lost every ounce of humanity, it should be known that the 911 emergency number is very much abused. I have responded to people calling 911 for hiccups, pimples, ingrown hairs, sneezing, pregnancy tests, itchy genitalia, fingernails that were cut too short, toothaches, mosquito bites, minor sunburns, nightmares and a plethora of other nonsensical "emergencies". First responders do not have the ability to refuse treatment or transport to any patient. So, if you want to be evaluated by an emergency physician for your fingernails that you accidentally cut too short, we're obligated to offer you transport.

In my anecdotal experience, for every one hundred emergency calls you run on, fifty of them need to see a doctor, and twenty-five of those need to see a doctor quickly; twelve of those are urgent, and five of those are true life-and-death emergencies. Ask any emergency medical responder about their "B.S." calls, and I'm fairly confident my experience will be echoed. I would contribute these types of calls as the main culprit for compassion fatigue and early-onset burnout.

I started drinking more and more on my seldom days off to deal with the lingering stress that I was still carrying from my days on shift. I would wake up and pour a shot of whiskey or rum to accompany my breakfast.

I convinced Leigh-Ann that this was normal and that everyone in my field lived like this, after all, MOST did. I would get defensive every time she would voice a concern. I learned that if I blew up and was adamant that she was worrying over nothing then she would back down. I started drinking every day I was off. I would sit around on shift and fantasize about getting home and pouring me a tall Jack and Coke. It was the only way I felt I could relax, and my brain had me completely convinced that without alcohol I would be a stressed-out ball of fury. With the alcohol, however, I was still a stressed-out ball of fury, but at least with the buzz I didn't seem to care.

I hated the person I became over those years. The bathroom mirror, where I once did all my soul searching, became a reflection that I couldn't even look at. The running and exercising that always pulled me out of my funk was now a distant memory. At this point of my life, I was too tired and busy to even think about running or exercising. I accepted the cynical asshole I'd become. I didn't feel like I was even worthy of feeling different. I felt the only thing I was worthy of was another drink.

As I continued to deteriorate emotionally, I continued to pick up as many shifts as my worn-out body would allow. I continued exposing myself to the worst humanity has to offer. The robotic voices of my dispatchers were unyielding.

"Medic 35, we need you en route to a possible overdose."

"Medic 35, we need you en route to a possible pediatric drowning."

"Medic 35, we need you en route to a possible gunshot wound."

"Medic 35, we need you en route to a possible sexual assault."

"Medic 35, we need you en route to a possible suicide."

"Medic 35, we need you en route to a possible cardiac arrest – CPR in progress."

"Medic 35, we need you en route to a motor vehicle accident."

"Medic 35, we need you en route to a possible stabbing."

"Medic 35, we need you en route to a possible domestic assault injury."

"Medic 35, we need you en route to a possible fall from a fourth story balcony."

"Medic 35, we need you en route to a possible alcohol-related issue."

"Medic 35, we need you en route to a possible gang-related assault."

"Medic 35, we need you en route to a possible object stuck in lower G.I. orifice."

"Medic 35, we need you en route to a possible…"

"Medic 35, we need you en route…"

"Medic 35, we need you…"

"Medic 35…"

"Medic 35…"

"Medic 35…"

IT WAS NEVER-ENDING! 911 calls penetrated my ears and irked my soul, similar to Christmas cheer and the Grinch. It was all noise, noise, noise, noise.

As my exposure to more and more calls increased, so did my desire to be numb. I finally reached the point that every emotion outside of my numb homeostasis was interpreted by my anxious brain as overwhelming. If I had a good day, I DRANK. If I had a bad day, I DRANK. If I was excited about something happening in my life, I DRANK.

My response to every situation was, yep, you guessed it, I… DRANK.

I knew the course I was on was unsustainable, as were most of the paths that I navigated. The fear of what the future held was one of my biggest anxieties at the time. Alas, this type of consternation became almost second nature to me, so integrated at my core that I didn't know where my anxiety started and reality stopped.

My body was also falling apart. I was in my early twenties but had the back, neck and knee pain of a well-seasoned sixty-five-year-old. I seemed to live with a constant dull headache, most likely due to the continual state of dehydration I lived in.

Overall, I always felt like I was just hit by a very slow-moving but very dense truck. I felt slow, lethargic and heavy. My diet mainly consisted of fast food and quick meals I could scarf down on the run. My stomach acids would bubble up into my throat, causing nausea-inducing indigestion. To sum it all up, I was a wreck.

I knew that I would need to find a new way of dealing with stress soon. The thought of no longer drinking was frightening, but the thought of digging up all the trauma I'd seen and poorly processed was nothing short of terrifying.

I got lost in tomorrow. I would always tell myself, *tomorrow, I'll reduce drinking, tomorrow, I'll start eating better*, or my personal favorite, *tomorrow, I'll deal with this*.

The problem for me was that "tomorrow" was a concept and not so much a time reference. "Tomorrow" signified a fantastical point in time when I would finally be ready to look at my own reflection again and take an honest inventory of the areas I was not happy with. I was stuck, frozen in fear and self-loathing. How could I possibly start to itemize areas that I wanted to change when I had developed such a deep-seated hate for the entire package? I never felt worthy of a rescue, but little did I know I was on the cusp of total freedom.

Part 3

Liberation

The day I was liberated from myself is a day that will forever be burned into my brain. I'm not sure how my brain stumbled upon the idea or how the seed was even planted, but during a normal, mundane shift I found the missing ingredient that seemed to give me the happiness I was so desperately searching for.

We were dispatched to a standard arm fracture. The patient presented in a lot of pain and nervousness. He was not only worried about the injury, but his anxiety due to having no medical insurance was skyrocketing. I tried to calm him down with words, but they fell on deaf ears. During transport I gave the patient a low dose of morphine to ease the pain. Instantly the patient went from tense, wincing and panicking to relaxed and calm.

Now, at this point in my career, I had given hundreds of patients doses of opiate narcotics, morphine, fentanyl and Dilaudid, for pain management, but for some reason this one was different. My brain was hyper-aware of the soothing reaction the drug gave the current patient I was treating. My eyes took special note of the physical alleviation produced by the magical concoction. I noticed how the patient seemed to take a deep breath and ease into the stretcher. He relaxed all of his muscles that were tense from pain and seemed to be in complete relief. This was a physical reaction that I would come to dub as the "morphine melt".

I watched as all the stress, worry and pain melted right off my patient. My brain was envious. It would happily trade the physical burden and pain of a broken arm for what appeared to be complete relaxation in a heartbeat.

At this point, a seed that was apparently dormant in my brain exploded and instantly took root. I can't recall exactly how long after that patient or exactly where the medication came from; I guess none of that is really important. The only important thing is, one day after shift, I found myself standing in my bathroom at home with an IV started, learning to experience the "morphine melt" first-hand.

THE EFFECTS WERE IMMEDIATE AND INTENSE!

I felt a warmness penetrate my calloused exterior and absorb quickly into the numb void within. I felt a blanket of warmth overcome my entire body as the tension in my shoulders, neck and jaw started to relax. The hairs on my arms stood up as my body adjusted to the feeling; this was similar to the type of feeling one would get when entering a hot tub and allowing your internal temperature to adjust.

I slowly moved my head to the right and left as my neck cracked and popped with each motion. My tension and tightness were gone. I took a deep breath and looked over the sink into the mirror and noticed my constricted pupils and relaxed brow.

This feeling was amazing. I felt happiness and relaxation to a level that I had never experienced prior. I felt like I could take on the world now that all my stress was gone. To some people, morphine and other opiates cause them to feel nauseous or extremely sleepy. For me however, it was like injecting pure unadulterated happiness. As if God himself came down and kissed my brain. I had a huge burst of energy and felt focused for the first time in a very long time.

I took a few moments while standing in my bathroom to bask in the radiant ambiance of the happiness that was quickly soaking into me. I finished up in the bathroom by hiding all IV supplies very carefully before heading out to meet Leigh-Ann and Hannah, still feeling absolutely amazing.

I'm not sure what took Leigh-Ann by surprise more, the fact that I didn't go directly for the liquor as per usual or the fact that my voice was upbeat and positive after a shift. Either way, we had a great day without me having a drop of liquor.

Did I mention that I felt AMAZING? Because I felt amazing!

I knew in the front of my mind that this stuff was one hundred percent more effective than the alcohol that was eroding away my esophagus and stomach, but in my soul, I knew that it was one thousand times darker. I also understood that there have been many people that have had their lives destroyed by the very stuff I was flirting with. At that point it didn't matter. My brain was finally awake and happy. The needle had my full attention.

I convinced myself that I was different from your "typical" drug addict. I thought I was special and above addiction, as if my alcohol use wasn't indicative enough of an addictive personality. I knew that I would never be the stereotypical drug addict that you see portrayed in Hollywood: in my young, arrogant mind they were weak. The morphine gave me a boldness that eased me into an instant complacency and whispered into my ear, "Not you, baby, you are different."

My pride signed a check that my willpower just couldn't fund.

I told myself that I needed to "pace" myself, and if I didn't get greedy, I could have an ongoing supply for as long as I wanted it. Even though I was new to this type of feeling, it was obvious that I needed to take it slow.

That strategy fell apart on my very next shift and seemed to continue to worsen at an unexpected rate.

Within about two weeks of my first use, I went from wanting to pace myself to actively looking for situations when I could score opiates. I would use my freshly-acquired score to offer up as a tribute to my depression-shriveled brain. It seemed to be the only thing that could breathe life into me.

The time flew by, with weeks turning into months, as weeks tend to do, and my scheme for obtaining opiates became more refined. It was a game… a game with the ultimate reward: abatement from a broken mind and escape from the crippling depression which I referred to as "life".

It seemed as if I had found the miracle key that I had been missing. My alcohol consumption dropped to nearly zero and I had more energy and pep to share with my family. The razor-sharp edge to my personality was now dulled by my sense of joy.

On the outside, it seemed as if I had finally followed through with my empty promises to reduce drinking that I had made so many times to Leigh-Ann. In reality, I had traded what seemed like a weekend love affair with alcohol, that I enjoyed on my few days off, for a full-time mistress that turned out to be demanding and cruel… her name was Addiction.

I quickly learned that morphine did not have the same negative effects on me as alcohol.

Alcohol always seemed to keep me comfortably numb. It didn't bring me happiness, it just made me not care about my sadness. It always brought with it a terrible feeling of remorse and embarrassment. It was very difficult to continue to explain and argue away my drinking with Leigh-Ann. It was very obvious to everyone around me that I had a drinking problem, except me.

I was so convinced that I was able to keep the effects of my drinking low key, meaning I didn't think anyone could tell just how drunk I was. I was undoubtedly convinced that I was "maintaining".

I was always humiliated to learn just how obvious my stupor was the following day when my wife would replay the previous night's events and discussions. I would argue that she was blowing the events out of proportion, until my brain would piece broken memories of the night's events together. I would remember just enough to realize she was right. I would immediately hang my head and apologize, followed by empty promises to reduce my drinking.

Leigh-Ann named my alter-drinking-ego the "Drunken Stupor", and it was fitting. At the time, I thought it was one big joke. I would tease her that the Drunken Stupor was a superhero and Richard was his Clark Kent. Looking back, it wasn't funny at all. What I viewed as a light-hearted superhero joke, Leigh-Ann viewed as a villain who was constantly stealing her husband from her and holding him hostage.

Morphine, on the other hand, was a stark contrast. She was amazing. She didn't just mask my sadness, she completely removed it. Morphine unleashed an exuberance in me that I never knew existed, I started feeling better instantaneously. It was the first time in years that I didn't crave alcohol in any capacity. It was almost like in my new reality, alcohol didn't even exist.

Morphine also had less negative physical effects on my body. I was no longer waking up feeling like I had gone ten rounds with my bed in the middle of the night. I was no longer waking up dry-heaving until my chest hurt and stomach spasmed. My acid reflux basically disappeared. The cotton mouth that morphine would leave was leading me to drink more and more water. My stomach reacted like the desert during a flash flood. I'm surprised that my gut even remembered how to absorb water with the embarrassing amounts I had been providing it over the years.

I started feeling great physically. My neck, back and knees were no longer throbbing in pain. My ongoing dull headache was no longer in play. I lost roughly twenty pounds the first month after ceasing my alcohol intake.

Although my physical improvements were drastic, my mental health benefits were even more apparent.

I was happy!

I wasn't only "not sad" but I was "truly happy". Morphine unlocked a deep and exaggerated empathetic response. I was beyond patient and understanding. I would interact with Leigh-Ann and Hannah and bring myself to tears because of how lucky I felt to have them in my life. This was always a feeling that I had deep down, but the morphine allowed these feelings to surface. Morphine seemed to magnify every positive feeling one could feel.

I no longer dreaded going to work: I actually looked forward to it. My desire to help others was reinvigorated and I was beyond willing to make and keep my patients comfortable and happy.

Leigh-Ann was beside herself. She was so happy to not only see the "old Richard" back but the new and improved Richard 2.0. It seemed as if the Drunken Stupor had finally hung up his cape.

She was elated when I dumped the remaining liquor in our house down the sink. I told her never again; I was taking my life back. I made multiple bold declarations about me no longer leaning on a chemical to ease my emotions, all the while knowing damn well that I had another dose of my bewitching mistress ready to shoot up right after my hollow speech.

Leigh-Ann had no idea what was going on behind the closed bathroom door. The bathroom mirror soon transformed from a place where I would take an honest inventory of myself to the reflection of a mad scientist experimenting with different chemicals. I no longer cared what the reflection in the mirror looked like or thought; after all, I had the keys to an alternate universe. A universe that, no matter what was happening in my life, I could escape to with the simple push of a syringe plunger.

For a while, I thought I had finally brought peace to my life. I would come to find out that my life was actually in pieces and becoming more fragmented with every injection of that bitch.

Reader Rescue: "Tomorrow" is an easy state of mind to get lost in. If you find yourself reading these pages and realizing that you are struggling with any type of substance abuse or mental health issues, stop reading and please locate some help. Do not be like me, allowing yourself to be so focused on "tomorrows" that you are losing your todays.

Chapter Seven

Part 1

Losing Bliss

"I was more addicted to self-destruction than to the drugs
themselves... something very romantic about it."
- Gerard Way

I was lost. I had no idea where I was or who I was. Not in the
literal sense, but when I looked at my shaking, blood-spotted
hand and pale, diaphoretic face in the filthy 7Eleven bathroom
mirror, I couldn't help but ask the questions:
Who am I?
And
How did I get here?
I was a complete mess. The honeymoon phase of my
euphorically charged opiate love affair was over. I was now
staring at the very thing I had so confidently promised myself
that I was incapable and above becoming... a drug addict.
My hands were shaking and my grip on the needle was
unsteady. The back of my hand was covered in bloody dots
from failed IV attempts. I was growing more and more
impatient and frustrated with every failed stick. My mind was

screaming at me, *STOP FUCKING AROUND AND GET IT INTO A VEIN, WE HAVEN'T GOT ALL DAY!*

As I steadied my breathing and held my breath, I felt the tip of the needle slide through my skin like a warm knife through butter. I felt a slight tension press against the end of the needle as the razor-sharp tip popped and penetrated through one of the only suitable veins I had left.

EUREKA!

I saw a flash of my own dark blood fill the syringe and I knew I was in. I steadied my hand even further as I slowly released the tourniquet and prepared to empty the contents of the syringe directly into my vascular system.

Within three seconds I could feel the ease of the drug take over my body. I felt the warm, familiar rush pervade my entire being. Suddenly, I no longer cared that I was desperately shooting up in a gas station bathroom in the middle of the night or that I resembled a sewer rat that dragged its trash to a festering private area to ingest its garbage.

I didn't care.

I just didn't care…

I no longer cared that I was the type of person I had vowed to never become. All I cared about was the next time I was able to be intimate with my seducer. All I cared about was the numbness rushing over me. All I cared about was not feeling like me. If that meant I had to be likened to a sewer rat for a few moments before complete relief, so be it.

I cleaned myself up and carefully disposed of my supplies. I wrapped my blood-soiled paper towels and used IV materials in clean paper towels and wet them. This made a wet paper ball with a biohazard core. I placed the wad into the garbage can and threw clean crumpled-up paper towels on top. I knew no one in their right mind would go digging through a gas station trash can – after all, I would be hard pressed to think of a more disgusting setting for someone to rummage through.

I washed off all the dried blood from the failed sticks on the back of my hand and arm. I always used the smallest needles I had available for two reasons: minimal bleeding and no track marks.

I grabbed my radio from the hook on the back of the bathroom door and headed back out to meet my partner, who was waiting for me in the ambulance.

Oh yeah… I almost forgot to tell you: I was on shift.

I crawled back into the ambulance and buckled up. My partner was impatiently sitting in the driver seat, waiting to ask me, "What the hell took so long?"

I told him indignantly, "I had to blow it up. Would you rather me wait until we got back to the station or do it here?"

We both laughed and off we went. We were on our way back to the station from the hospital when I decided I needed a "morphine meet-up". I asked him to pull into the 7-Eleven because my stomach was upset. He obliged and here we were.

As we made our way back to the station, a dispatcher came across the radio, "Medic 35…"

I responded, "Go ahead for Medic 35…"

They asked, "What's your location?"

I responded with the exact intersection we were stopped at.

A few moments of silence went by, and the emergency tones dropped.

"Medic 35, Medic 35, we need you en route for a possible man down." They then proceeded to give us the exact location of the call and off we went.

We arrived at a very nice house located in a prominent side

of town. We were met at the front door by a middle-aged woman, who informed us that her brother had been in the shower for a long time and was not answering her knocks on the door. She went on to inform us that he had recently been diagnosed with diabetes and his sugar levels had been up and down recently.

We walked to the bathroom door and knocked sternly. No answer. We made multiple attempts to jiggle the old-school doorknob open, to no avail. My partner dropped to his stomach and peeked under the door. He reported that he saw what looked like someone laying on the ground. We told the sister that we could wait for the responding fire engine, which was about five minutes away, to arrive and use the proper tools to take the door down, or we could kick it in. Panicking, she responded, "Kick the damn thing down!"

My partner and I squared up with the door and channeled our inner Dog the Bounty Hunter. We both quickly counted down out loud, three... two... one. As we both booted the door in a synchronized and precise attack, we heard the door frame crack as the solid wood started to splinter on the other side. We recovered and counted down again, three... two... one. We both kicked forward with an even stronger force than the first kick. The door frame then completely split, and the door flew open in a burst of splintered frame.

The force of my kick kept my momentum moving forward, as the door no longer absorbed it. My foot flew forward, landing on the linoleum bathroom floor in a puddle of unexpected blood. Slipping forward, my partner caught me and helped me regain my balance. Within a fraction of a second, we realized what had happened to the patient.

His body was laying on the cold bathroom floor in a

swimmable puddle of his own blood. We immediately noticed that the body was headless and caught sight of the shotgun lying next to him on the bathroom floor. The shower curtain directly behind the patient was painted red with blood and peppered with buckshot that went on to shatter and penetrate the tiled wall. The room had a thin haze of red to it from the blood droplets that were still drifting about. I noticed a section of the lower jaw that was sitting on the bathroom counter with teeth still in place.

After what seemed like a lifetime of staring at and absorbing this gruesome scene, when in reality it was maybe two to three seconds, we exited the doorway, grabbing the sister before she had a chance to catch a glimpse. We quickly guided her out of the house to the front porch. She demanded that we tell her what was happening with an increasingly alarmed voice.

Both my partner and I were unable to even speak, let alone find the words to describe what we had seen.

"There's nothing we can do," my partner let out through a shaken, mousy voice.

Further, I tried to explain that his injuries were too severe for us to work on and that there was nothing we could do.

She cried out in a blast of emotional confusion and tried to push her way past us. We wrapped her up just as her knees were giving out. She collapsed to the porch bench and wailed in grief, asking what had happened.

I stepped away to give our dispatch and responding fire engine an update.

I informed dispatch that we were "Signal 7", which is radio speak for dead on arrival.

"We are currently on scene with what appears to be a self-inflicted shotgun wound to the head. His injuries are incompatible with life; no CPR in progress. We are currently providing emotional care and support to an on-scene family member," I said robotically.

The sister overheard my update to dispatch and her cries for understanding intensified as she struggled to catch her breath.

Suddenly, it hit me... my high was gone. I no longer felt the sweet embrace of numbness. I started to feel real emotions. My brain started to panic as it felt the real world crashing in on it. I know I should have felt grief for the patient's sister, who was falling apart directly in front of us, or sorrow for the patient himself. He had digressed to a point in his life that a loaded shotgun in the mouth was more appealing than continuing on with life.

Sadly, all I felt in that moment was panic... panic that I had just lost my high and would be faced with the real world. Panic because I had no idea how much longer I would be stuck on scene and unable to meet up with my temptress, morphine. Finally, panic because I knew that this man's suicide SHOULD have had some type of effect on me, but regretfully all I could focus on was my own selfish "problems".

I stood on scene as the fire engine, multiple law enforcement officers and my captain arrived. I watched it all blankly as I stared past the action that seemed to be moving in slow motion around me. My panic morphed into something even more insidious as I stood there. Anger seemed to creep in and took explosive growth, consuming my every thought.

How stupid is this that I'm stuck here with literally nothing to do?

This... is... RIDICULOUS...

How much longer?

Jesus Christ! Can we hurry this up!

My mind was on fire, burning with deep self-absorption and the fantasy of retreating back into myself with a little help from the needle. I started to sweat as thoughts like these consumed my inner soul.

Just as I was about to crack and scream with impatience, I watched as the coroner drove up.

FINALLY, my mind celebrated in a soft voice of consolation.

I knew that this call was finally wrapping up. As I refocused on the action that was going on around me, I realized that the sister's emotional status had completely collapsed. She was a wreck. It turned out that their parents had also died just months before, and her brother was her only family left. She was inconsolable and unable to even react to basic commands.

Everyone decided that transport to the emergency department was best. She was in the middle of a complete nervous breakdown and had no one who could be with her after we left. I was completely quiet during the decision-making process; I was silently hoping that she would pull it together so as to not delay me from my date with the morphine I had on me.

After we loaded up and started towards the hospital, I was hyper-aware of the saving grace. I could feel the vial pressing and resting against my outside thigh as it sat in my pocket like a latent salvation.

I administered some Valium to the patient to ease her anxiety, at the direction of the receiving physician. I was envious of the relief she displayed. It was only a matter of time before I could enjoy my own personal relaxation.

By the time we arrived at the hospital, I had one thing on

my mind: myself.

I dropped the patient off and provided the receiving nurse with a verbal hand-off report. Through a very uninfluenced and apathetic voice, I bid the patient good luck and apologized for her loss. To this day, I am crushed by just how insincere and automated I was.

As I made my way out of the Emergency Department, I noticed an open and empty staff restroom. The thought occurred, *Why risk the chance of getting another call by going to a gas station restroom, when I could just shoot up here before even going back in service?*

I made my way back out to the ambulance to grab the materials from my personal bag that I would need before heading back into the hospital. I entered the staff restroom and set up my materials. My brain raced with excitement. It was time. I removed the vial of morphine from my pocket as carefully as a man of God would handle ancient holy scrolls. I took a few moments to get my mind right to enjoy the salvation to the maximum.

As I drew up the liquid, I noticed that my viewpoint of it seemed to change. I no longer viewed it as a secret love affair but more as a deep yearning that satisfied my soul. I no longer felt that this was a fun fling but more like an actual part of me that I required to function. This was no longer a mistress; this was an all-out deity to me now.

The morphine was my god, the needle my minister and the bathroom my temple.

I remember that this thought shook me completely. I knew that not only had I crossed a line, but I now found myself so far past the line that it appeared to be a dot to me.

My brain said sarcastically, as I slid the needle into the

back of my hand, *well, I'm already here, might as well enjoy it.*

It was time to worship, and I never wanted to pass up the opportunity to allow the spirit to consume me.

I will never forget that day. It was the first time that I realized that this may be a problem down the road. I didn't care. With my new religion I could face anything. Sadly, I was on the brink of finding out just how merciless, vile, heinous and evil my new god was.

Part 2

~~Denomination~~
Domination

Nikki Sixx, the famous bassist for the iconic eighties rock band Mötley Crüe, once said, "Selling my soul would be a lot easier if I could just find it."

Even though my life was not one of stardom, fame and rock-n-roll, I completely sympathized with this statement. I HAD LOST MY SOUL. Let me rephrase, I WILLINGLY TRADED MY SOUL FOR THE FEELING OF COMFORT and a brief escape from the person I was.

I spent more and more time thinking of shooting up and strategizing ways to get more and more opiates. It wasn't enough for me just to be shooting up, I needed to know where my next high was coming from. I not only lost myself, but I also lost my reaction to the magic potion. I was no longer only getting high. I was mainly using it because I was anxious, and if I'm brutally honest, scared as hell to be without it. I put the "need" in the word needle.

I started experimenting with other drugs and slowly started drinking again. I learned what substance perpetuated the drugs to maximize my enjoyment of them. I tried everything I could think of to restore the early-onset romance I had with morphine, but sadly it was a fleeting feeling that I would never be able to recreate.

I started popping Adderall pills like candy. Adderall is a prescription stimulant that acts like a bolt of lightning to your central nervous system. It is typically used to treat ADHD in children and adults. It helps people who are struggling with their attention span to focus and calms them down. It is an amphetamine and closely mimics the same feelings as meth. I learned first-hand that if I crushed the pill down and snorted the powder, its effects were a lot stronger and immediate. It filled me with energy and focus to take higher quantities of opiates, which acted like a buffer to even me out.

I learned that if I drank a bottle of Nyquil right after shooting up, the diphenhydramine would intensify the effects of the morphine.

I was no longer happy with my new religion. It was no longer fun, new and exciting. It seemed to twist and contort into something very dark, something depraved. I no longer recognized myself. I know this seems to be a familiar story, but this time was different. This time my reflection held no resemblance of my former self.

Looking into the mirror, my eyes were empty and seemed to stare forward with the blankness of a thousand yards. I was present, but I was not there. Every time in the past, when I found myself not liking the man looking back at me, I had an emotional reaction to it. I was driven to fight and claw my way back to be the person I wanted to be. The scariest part was now I no longer cared. I was completely detached and disassociated from myself. I not only had zero desire to fight my way back to being the man I was proud of, I didn't feel like I deserved anything but this void. I felt utterly alone inside and worse, I convinced myself I deserved it.

My ambition was gone.

My pride was gone.

My self-respect was gone.

My soul was gone.

The only positive thing that remained was love for my family. My love was still very much alive and well. I loved Leigh-Ann and Hannah more than anything in the world. Looking back, I can honestly say that my love for those two girls never changed or wavered. They were the only positives in my life.

I despise the person I was during this time period. Leigh-Ann was watching the man she loved shrivel up into a hardened cocoon of depression and anxiety.

Leigh-Ann is a very intelligent and sharp individual, a lot sharper than I am. It wasn't long after starting to use morphine that she started noticing little things that seemed off. Mainly, how long I would take in the restroom and my personality shift after exiting. She had her suspicions, but I was very cunning when it came to leaving no concrete evidence that she could use against me.

Every time she would ask me what was going on, I would act like I had no idea what she was talking about. I would try to make her seem insane while quickly blowing up, in hopes she would back down.

For this, Leigh-Ann, I am so sorry.

My sanity was quickly slipping away. I would go to work, perform the motions and go home. I was no longer the personable paramedic I used to be. I no longer enjoyed my job or being around people. It's not that I didn't like people, it's that I felt completely empty and unable to harbor any emotions towards anyone. I felt incapable of having feelings. I was completely apathetic when I was high and completely angry when the drugs started wearing off. It was an emptiness that was indescribable and engulfing.

I felt like a functional mausoleum: strong on the outside but filled with death on the inside. It was a hopelessness that I wouldn't wish on my worst enemy. I found myself living needle prick to needle prick with nothing but remorse, shame and anxiety in between each insertion.

I lost all my self-respect and self-esteem. I felt unworthy to have such a wonderful family. My emotional rollercoaster continued to dictate the temperament and disposition of the house. I wanted to be left alone because I felt that I didn't deserve love and attention, but then I also desperately craved time with my family. It was a very strange head space to occupy.

The feeling of impending collapse was imminent. Every day I woke up wondering if today was the day everything was going to fall apart. I lived in a constant state of anxiety and worry, as if I were walking around with a bomb strapped to my chest, just waiting for the right conditions to explode.

Like a rock constantly beaten by the elements and slowly broken down, I developed a fragility and took on a whole new shape, a shape that would not support the ever-growing pressure and abuse from my elected elements. A rock slide was coming and it wasn't going to be pretty. I just hoped that it wouldn't reduce me to a useless pile of rubble.

Part 3

Martyrdom

"Medic 35... Medic 35, we need you code 3 for an unresponsive pediatric."

Once again, my dispatcher's voice broke through the calm night air as the emergency tones followed like thunder to lightning.

I rolled out of my bunk and quickly reached for my pants and boots. I grabbed the half-empty energy drink off my nightstand and headed out to the bay where my partner would meet me at the ambulance.

I gulped the room-tepid energy drink to freshen up my middle-of-the-night breath.

I quickly slugged my way to my ambulance, loaded up and placed us in a "responding" status.

My dispatcher came back over the airwaves to inform me that we were responding to a one-month-old who was found unresponsive while sleeping.

Yes, you read that right...

"Unresponsive WHILE sleeping."

That was the description of the complaint we received before rolling out.

Completely ridiculous.

Once we arrived on scene, we made our way to the front door, where we were met by a panicking man in his mid-thirties, who was clearly trying to hide the worry he had brewing internally.

He quietly and quickly escorted us through his upper-middle-class home to the nursery, where we found the baby patient being rocked by his mother. He was swaddled tightly and appeared to be sleeping while mom rocked him vigorously and hummed at a stressed intensity. As I made eye contact with mom, I could see tears welling in her eyes alongside panic and anguish.

As I approached hesitatingly, I could tell that the baby was not sleeping. His stillness was too profound to be asleep. The feeling hit the pit of my stomach as I reached out to take him into my arms. As I stared into the breathless, lifeless face, my breath was ripped from my chest. He was a complete enigma to me… a sort of violent placidity.

He looked so peaceful, swaddled with care and gently resting in my arms. The ferocity of his peacefulness afflicted me deeply. While holding him in my arms, my brain strived to find the subtle shift of breath entering and leaving his little body. I was clinging onto a false hope that my eyes were lying to me. He was gone.

I refocused my eyes and noted the ashen-gray skin on his face and the deep purples that made up his ears and neck.

Within less than a second of him being in my arms, I realized he had not only passed away, but he had been gone for a while, hours even. There was nothing that we could do.

Just as I was coming to that realization, I noticed mom's face. She was frantically staring at mine, hoping I would look up and tell her everything was okay and that this was all just a bad dream. I could see that the next words I spoke were going to have an everlasting effect on her.

As I struggled to put together a tapestry of words to gently tell her that her son was dead, I watched as the dark realization seeped through her face. I witnessed her struggle to remember how to breathe as she dropped to her knees and started a guttural scream-cry.

I glanced over to my partner, who was also paralyzed in the moment. I knew we had to act. We had to do SOMETHING...

Within about four to five seconds of having the baby placed in my arms, we were in full-on first responder mode. At this point, we knew we were not treating the baby – there was nothing we could do.

At this point, we were treating mom and dad. I decided to work this baby just as hard as I would work a viable child. I never wanted the parents to look back at this pivotal moment and think that we did not do all we could to help him. After all, I knew there was nothing we could do, but how do you look a brand-new mother in the eye and explain that there is no hope?

NO! When she looked back at this moment in time, she was going to know that we DID EVERYTHING WE COULD.

We promptly got to work. We made our way to the ambulance as the fire engine crew was pulling up. I grabbed the paramedic from that crew and quickly and discreetly said, "We're working him for mom and dad."

We were instantly on the same page. We gathered the gear needed and took off to the hospital. We allowed mom to ride in the front while dad followed. I knew mom was watching everything we were doing, and I made sure she knew we were working hard for any chance possible.

I radioed the receiving hospital and discreetly let them know the situation. They said they would be ready when we arrived.

As we pulled up, we were met at the door by a nurse and physician. They briskly escorted us to the assigned room. Upon entering, there were two more nurses and a chaplain, who walked to meet mom. They took over care and made it known that everyone wanted the best for this baby.

As I exited, I noticed the chaplain trying to console mom in the hallway. I tried to avoid her, but she locked eyes with me. She quickly approached me and the other paramedic and collapsed in our arms. She wrapped her arms around our necks and sobbed. Her legs buckled, and we were basically holding her up in the hallway. The chaplain and a nurse helped peel her off us and assisted her to a chair. We then saw fit to make our way back to the ambulance.

As we were cleaning up the truck, the charge nurse and another physician came out to ask us more questions about what had happened. I explained the scene in its entirety and started to explain my rationale for my decision to work him. After hearing the cracking hesitation in my voice, the physician interrupted me and said that I had done the right thing and she would have done the same. This brought a little closure to the gaping hole that I felt in my heart.

After dropping the medic from the fire crew off at his station, we returned to ours. I headed into my bunk room with my head held low. My partner struggled to find the words to express his support and encourage me. He awkwardly blundered through the offer to talk if I needed to. He was an awesome guy, and I knew he would do his best to sincerely listen if I needed to unload, but the problem was I couldn't find the words to describe the ever-dense hole that was expanding inside me.

I thanked him for his offer, but I just wanted to isolate myself. I waited in my bunk room until I heard the TV from the living area turn off and his bunk room door close. I quietly made my way to the restroom with my IV supplies in hand.

I found myself standing in front of the mirror, setting up my supplies on a sterile field on top of the sink. I glanced up at my reflection and noticed my shirt was still wet from the mom's tears.

How could this be? I pondered as I realized that it had been roughly an hour and a half since her collapse in the hallway.

I quickly realized that the dampness was not from the mother who fell into our arms. This tear-soaked shirt was from my own supply. I was so disassociated with everything about this call that I didn't even notice that I had maintained a steady stream of tears since departing the hospital.

As soon as I came to terms with the emotional impact of that call, I lost it. I started uncontrollably crying and hyperventilating. I struggled with shaking hands to finish off starting my IV. I trembled as I pulled up the Dilaudid in the fresh syringe and attached it to the IV. I pushed the plunger of the syringe as quickly as I could, rushing the drug into my system with haste.

I felt the poison rush my mind and quickly take control. I felt the calming effect take hold immediately and I was able to bring myself out of my emotional low. I glanced back at myself in the mirror, noting the puffy red eyes with the dark circles underneath, my belly that was bulging over my belt once again, the greasy appearance on my unkempt face and the overall grunginess of my disheveled appearance.

I looked deep into my reflection and noticed how dead I

appeared behind the eyes. I was nowhere to be found in the mirror.

I was done.

It was at that moment, in that bathroom, after that call, I decided that I no longer wanted to live.

I had been flirting with the passive thoughts of no longer dealing with life for a while. My self-esteem was so broken that I was convinced that Leigh-Ann and Hannah would be better off without me. I was a complete waste of human life, in my own lifeless eyes. I wanted to check out. I wanted all the numbness and anger to be over.

I hated the idea that I was a drug addict and alcoholic. I hated the fact that I "knew" I was keeping Leigh-Ann and Hannah from living their best lives with the emotional baggage I constantly carried. The most frustrating aspect was that I couldn't even put to words what was wrong with me. My depression was so widespread throughout my entire being that I didn't distinguish the issues in me. I felt that I as a whole was the issue.

I left the bathroom and called my shift commander. I told him that I was not in the right headspace to be on shift. I told him that the baby shook me up and I needed to go home. He didn't ask too many follow-up questions. I think it was understandable that this type of call would take a part of anyone's soul. He took my ambulance out of service until he found coverage and allowed me to leave.

I arrived home and lost it. I sat in my car, crying. I could feel the tears roll down my numb exterior and soak into my still-damp shirt. I convinced myself that this life was not worth it… I convinced myself that I was not worth it. I grabbed a bottle of Dilaudid from my bag and went inside. I softly kissed Hannah on her forehead and tucked her in tighter. I quietly entered my bedroom and found Leigh-Ann fast asleep in a peaceful rest. She looked like an angel, which affirmed my suspicion that I did not deserve her. I kissed her on the forehead and entered our bathroom.

I stood in front of our mirror and grimaced at the person looking back. I was a million miles from myself. I was lost with no sense of direction back to a person I could respect. I had no inner north star to guide me; inside my head there was only a black vacuum. A vacuum that extended to my heart and devoured my soul.

I crushed down the remaining pills I had in my bottle and melted them down. It yielded a dose that was about ten times the amount that I typically used. A dose that would finally give me the true numbness I felt I deserved. I'm not sure if I really wanted to die or felt that it was just the next step in the progression of my downfall.

I was so confused.

As I drew up my liquefied exit strategy, my hands trembled and shook with anticipation. I knew this would be it: I would either have the best high of my life or I would die. Either way it was a win-win situation.

The sweat and tears dripped down my face as I attempted to start the IV that would deliver my atonement. I pushed the needle head through the back of my hand at my typical IV site. The moment the needle touched the outside of the vein, the vein exploded under my skin. The site swelled up as the blood collected under the surface.

Shit!

Well, that site's blown.

I attempted my second and third go to site. Every time I tried to start the IV, the same thing would happen. I continued to fish for a vein that I could access, but every attempt resulted in a failure. My brain taunted me.

Could it be possible that I was such a complete fuck up that I couldn't even kill myself?

I grew more and more aggravated and started inserting the needle even more aggressively, which in return would cause the veins to blow even faster.

I must have stuck myself forty times before becoming so aggravated that I gave up and dropped to my knees. I internally cried out as the dots of blood trickled down my hands, arms, legs, feet and the left side of my neck, where I had attempted to access my jugular vein.

WHY?
WHY AM I HERE?
WHY WON'T YOU JUST LET ME GO?
WHY DO YOU HATE ME?
WHAT THE HELL DO YOU WANT FROM ME?

I had no idea who I was crying out to. Maybe it was myself, or maybe it was the remembrance of a belief in a God that I had long forgotten. All I knew was there must be a reason greater than myself that I was still breathing. It was the first time in years that I felt a strange feeling of hope and purpose.

As I lay on that cold bathroom floor, I stared at the ceiling and took a mental inventory of the mess that I called my life. I needed to change but had no clue where to start.

Then it dawned on me.

I can start right here, right now.

I picked myself up and looked in the mirror

I hoisted myself back up to my knees, grasping the edge of

my sink counter. I lifted my trembling body back up to my shaky feet and looked at my reflection.

My overwhelming sadness morphed into a righteous anger with myself.

How did I let myself get to this point?

It was a question that I have contemplated with contempt many times in my life.

I picked the syringe up off the bathroom floor and studied the contents. I rolled the plastic cylinder between my fingers as I thought about my amazing wife, broken, telling Hannah that her daddy was gone. I thought about the emotional damage that I would be inflicting on those two wonderful souls.

I thought about Hannah growing up without a father to guide and protect her. I thought about her graduating without me being there to tell her how proud I was of her. I saw her, in my head, walking down the aisle at her wedding by herself without having a father arm in arm. I tortured myself with the idea that my decision may be the reason her life was completely derailed.

In a brief moment of courage and strength, I emptied the contents of that syringe down the sink drain. I gathered up all my IV supplies and threw them in the trash can outside. I jumped in the shower and washed the now dry and crusty blood off. I realized that the Dilaudid I had just wasted was all the opiates I had at the time. I told myself over and over that I was finished with drugs, and I would get myself together. I told myself this so much that I convinced myself that cold turkey was possible.

As I exited the shower, my wife entered the bathroom half-awake, inspecting what was going on in the brightly lit bathroom. Through teary and stressed eyes, I gave her a quick synopsis of the call. She hugged me and held me tight. I could feel my legs buckle as I lowered myself to the side of our tub. She continued to hold my head tightly against her chest in a loving and supportive embrace. As my tears soaked the t-shirt she was wearing as a nightshirt, I could hear the soft metronome of her heartbeat.

I instantly felt comfortable and at ease. Leigh-Ann was always and continues to be my safe space. As long as I am with her, I feel like everything will be all right. She had no idea of the turmoil that had just taken place in my head. She had no clue that this bathroom was the stage of the darkest moment of my hopeless life. All she knew was that I was struggling to keep it together. She sat there holding me for what seemed like an eternity.

Once I was able to gather myself, we went to bed. She wrapped her arms around me and snuggled into my back. At that moment, I knew that my life wasn't all pain.

The next morning, I woke up and told Leigh-Ann that we needed to talk. We sat down and I exploded with a free-flowing projectile stream of word vomit. I told her that I had a drug problem and that I needed help. Without telling her about my dance with the devil the night before, I told her how scared I was of myself and how I felt completely, utterly and absolutely hopeless. I explained how inadequate I felt as a person and how I felt she would be better off without me.

I watched as the tears and horror arose in her eyes. I tried to gauge whether these tears were from anger, disappointment or disgust. I quickly realized that the tears were from fear, love and the sincere desire to help me. I watched as the person I thought would be better off without me completely fell apart at just the thought of losing me. I observed as my confession and secret life ripped her heart out and threw it around the room.

Breaking down and telling the person I respected the most in the world that I was nothing, but a two-bit drug addict was by far the hardest conversation I have ever initiated. I was prepared for many responses, but not the one I received.

In keeping with her sweet and loving nature, she wrapped her arms around me and softly said, "We're going to get through this. You're the strongest man I know, and if anyone can come back from this, it's you."

The comfort and the warmth of her strong words, coupled with the sweet softness of her voice, radiated through me. Her presence and support instantaneously calmed the turbulence inside. I nestled into her neck and just allowed her to hold me. It was the first time in years that I allowed myself to be vulnerable without wearing my "tough guy" mask. It was a moment of pure, unadulterated love and support. It had been so long since I allowed myself to feel feelings that the emotions felt alien.

"I'm so lost right now. I have no idea how to even get back to being myself," I said with a sobbing voice.

Leigh-Ann responded with what may be the most profound advice I have ever received,

"By taking one step at a time."

Reader Rescue: Looking back at this time of my life, I passionately hate the person that I was. I had become a selfish, self-absorbed piece of shit. I was living my life with complete reckless abandonment and taking risks that no person should ever flirt with. I cannot thank God enough for the grace and mercy he showed me during these years. My life wasn't on its way to being a disaster, it was there. I should have asked for help a lot sooner, but my pride and fear of what other people thought crippled me and my belief that I didn't deserve help held me in place. I thank God every day that I never made a mistake on the job that ended in harm. There is nothing that anybody can say or think about me that is harsher than the judgement I cast on myself. To any person who was ever affected in any way by my mental health issues and substance abuse coping skills, I am sincerely and truly sorry.

Also, the one-month-old baby developed SIDS shortly after being placed down by his loving parents for the night.

Chapter Eight

Part 1

False Start

"You feel your strength in the experience of pain."
- Jim Morrison

Twenty-four hours after my complete breakdown, I found myself laying in my bed, struggling with the deepest shivers I have ever experienced. The violent shaking I was victim to forged in my core and rattled my entire body. These tremors put Leonardo DiCaprio's final scene from *Titanic* to shame. Although I felt as if I were dying, I was merely detoxing from the poisons that my body had become dependent on.

It had been years since I had gone without some type of substance to cope with the unmistakable truth of my self-awareness. I'm not particularly sure what was worse, losing my drugs or being reintroduced to the person I was avoiding for so many years.

I was forced to call off work for an entire week, while my body and mind was twisting and contorting on itself. I was bed-ridden for the first five days of the detoxification due to extreme back pain, leg cramps, nausea, vomiting and overall weakness. I found myself sleeping most of the time when I was not

throwing up or crying because of the intense emotional downs.
My lower back felt as if I had a vice grip squeezing every nerve ending and twisting with force. My kidneys felt as if they were turning inside out on themselves. My stomach ached as if I had been solely living on a diet of curdled milk for months leading to this moment.

Every muscle in my body pulsated in pain, and they felt like they were tenderized with a ball peen hammer. I was unable to lift my head off the pillow without creating a Charley horse in my neck and shoulders. Puking turned out to be one of the most involved issues I faced. Any time I would even take a sip of water or nibble of food, my body threw itself into violent, painful rejections.

Now, I've never been punched in the gut by Mike Tyson per se, but I cannot imagine a deeper penetrating gastric pain than detoxing off alcohol and opiates.

My mental health and emotions suffered the most. The five days I was stuck in bed I became completely unhinged. I was having both visual and auditory hallucinations and not the good kind. I swear, I was hearing the devil subtly whispering to me. I intently strained to listen to the slight whispering, in an attempt to make out what I was hearing. The textures on my wall started to move and intertwine like a slow-moving kaleidoscope. My dreams and nightmares were so vivid and violent that they bordered on breaking the Geneva Convention's restrictions on torture.

My wife waited on me hand and foot to make sure I had everything I needed in an attempt to achieve some level of comfort. She would wipe my head with a cool towel and change the sheets when I would saturate them with my sweat. She would turn the air down and turn on the fan when I was too warm and stacked blankets on top of me when I started to freeze. This temperament cycle of temperature intolerance would repeat roughly every fifteen to twenty minutes. Leigh-Ann would draw four to five warm baths with Epsom salts a day to help my sore muscles.

When she said, "By taking one step at a time", I had no idea that she would be the one carrying me through the first and most difficult steps.

Leigh-Ann would sit on the edge of the bed, hold my hand, and tell me how proud of me she was. Not only did she find time to take care of Hannah and shield her from seeing her father in that state, she also gracefully attended to the wreckage laying on my side of the bed. Her capacity for compassion is rivaled by none. As I write these pages, she is still the most selfless person I have ever met in my life.

On day six, I felt well enough to finally get up and get dressed. I had to get out of the house. I felt like the walls were closing in. We decided to take a drive up to a local shopping mall and stroll around. Leigh-Ann would be able to complete a few outstanding errands and I would be reintroduced to sunlight.

On our drive to the mall, Leigh-Ann praised me so much for making it through the last few days. Her amount of happiness and pride in me made me feel guilty and uncomfortable.

How could someone be so proud of someone for detoxing... I'm the one who chose to do the drugs. Why shouldn't I pay the price? I thought to myself.

I stayed quiet and let her talk. It seemed to make her feel better and gave her a sense of being in control to voice her pride in me. It's not that I wasn't thankful for her support; I still felt like I didn't deserve it.

I didn't respect myself. *Why should she?*

After arriving at the mall, we sauntered around from store to store until my legs and back started to cramp. I told Leigh-Ann that I just needed to sit down for a while and that she should finish her list before leaving. I decided to sit on a bench in a bookstore and wait for her.

After telling her that I would be fine approximately one hundred and fifty-seven times, she left with Hannah in the stroller. She told me she only had to go to two other stores, then she would be finished. I told her to take her time and I would be sitting here when she got back.

After she left, I decided to check out the magazine rack located directly in front of the bench. I noticed an issue of *Runner's World Magazine* with a subtitle that read, "How to get started."

I picked it up and returned to my bench. As I flipped through the pages, some nostalgic memories surfaced of training for my first 5k years earlier.

I'm not sure if it was the mental exhaustion, borderline delusion or the fact that I had actually survived my detox, but my emotions were still all over the place. I teared up at the memories of training and actually feeling proud of myself. Thumbing through the pages, I started to feel inspiration bubble up inside me.

I read the article with regard to "getting started". It spoke about starting slow and gradually building mileage. It took me back to my mailbox-to-mailbox fiasco that I had conquered in a distant past. I smiled at the thought of my first finish line crossing and instantaneously felt a strange pull in my heart. As I made it to the middle of the magazine, I opened it to a centerfold advertisement for the Walt Disney World Marathon. It read something along the lines of, "Join us for the happiest race on Earth!"

Even though it sounded cheesy, in the moment my brain clung to the word "happiest".

I thought back to my conversation with my partner Erik and how impressed I was by his mention of running the Jacksonville Marathon years before. I had a brief moment of insanity and thought, *Why can't I do that?*

Boom, the seed was planted.

Part 2

Ready... Set... Nope

After a couple of weeks of internal back and forth, I finally approached Leigh-Ann and asked what she thought about me starting to run again. She was so happy to hear a sign of motivation fall from my lips. I had been walking around the house despondent since my detox. I would leave to work my shift, white-knuckle my sobriety, drive home, white-knuckle some more and then repeat.

She was taken off-guard by my question but was very supportive and inquisitive about what my overall goal was. I told her, "I think I want to run the Walt Disney World Marathon."

She told me that she thought that was a great idea and she would support it anyway she could. After making that statement, she asked the question most non-runners ask.

"How long is it?"

I responded, "26.2 miles."

She repeated, "26.2," with a stressed and surprised voice.

Once she realized the tone she was conveying, she doubled down on her original stance of support.

She asked when it was, and I told her it was in January. I would have about six months to get in shape to run it. She went online that night, signed me up and presented it as my Father's Day gift.

Now, anyone who has ever run a Disney race knows they are not cheap. Leigh-Ann made a huge financial investment by signing me up. While I was detoxing, I had made a promise to cut my overtime significantly. With the hours lost, the pay followed suit. It didn't matter to her. It was a power move on her part to show that she was all in. Now, it was my turn to prove my drive.

The next day, I decided to go out for my first run in years. I quickly found the stark truth in the age-old saying, "If you don't use it, you lose it". I felt worse than I had when I first started running years earlier. My body was in complete rebellion mode and my mind was so fragile that it felt that it could break at any moment. I remembered my plan of attack that had worked for me years earlier and mimicked it. I took solace in the fact that I was running a familiar road.

The first few weeks I ran in place; not in the literal sense, but more in the sense that I felt as if I were making zero forward progress. My everyday performance seemed to be worse than the day before. My back cramped and spasmed with the effort of keeping me upright alone. My legs were heavy and slow, as if I were wearing cinder blocks as shoes. My mind seemed to unravel more and more with every step that I would push through.

Looking back, the mental aspects were by far the hardest to overcome. I broke the entire journey down into manageable steps. Even though I had a plan, every small goal that I set for myself always seemed secondary to my obsessions. As motivated and desperate as I was to complete the marathon distance, alcohol and opiates created a blinding obsession that stayed in the front of my mind. It was like I was standing in a dark tunnel and a speeding locomotive was heading my way.

Words cannot express how much I hated those substances, but strangely enough, it is equally hard to put to words how much I missed them.

During these weeks, my secret to sobriety was thick-headed stubbornness. Every day I woke up thinking that today would be the day that I relapsed. I was clinging to my sobriety like an inexperienced climber clinging to the side of Half Dome in a downpour. I found myself being solely powered by anger and rage. I was angry with myself, and I used my running as an outlet to rage against my addiction.

After persistent dedication and a ton of support from the home front, I started to see slight gains. My body was starting to adjust to the new exercise and the loss of its old addictive crutch. My nightmares and morning tremors dissipated, and I realized I was sleeping better at night. My back cramps, leg cramps and malaise subsided as well. My body was on the mend, but my mind was still on the fray. I did however notice slight gains to my emotional well-being as a result of the improvements in my runs. I also noticed my attitude was slightly more upbeat and optimistic.

With steady persistence and a willingness to take one step at a time, I was down thirty pounds and had the ability to run a 5k within two months. I was running multiple times every day.

After reaching the 5k mark, my progress seemed to explode like a Molotov cocktail of momentum. I quickly progressed from the 5k distance to four miles, then to five and then to six, with very little time in between.

Once I got to the 10k distance, it was just a short jump to the half-marathon distance. I made this leap with little perceived effort as I sailed through my training plan. I think this was partly due to the wrecked state I started running in. As my body started to heal, the perceived difficulty of my runs started to drop.

The anger and rage that fueled me to this point started to lose its edge. I couldn't help but have a glimmer of happiness in my heart and an old spark of hope in my soul.

At the four-month marker, I was able to consistently run thirteen to fifteen miles in a single effort. I started to feel proud of myself once again. I was so happy with my progress that I decided I deserved a reward.

I read an article online that promoted alcohol use during race training. I very quickly convinced myself that it wasn't really the alcohol that I had the issue with. I duped myself into agreeing that as long as I could stay off the needle and pills, I would be able to control my drinking and drink like a normal person... no, a normal runner.

During my runs, I incorporated fantasizing about being the runner who crossed the finish line and cracked open a cold beer or toasted a shot glass of liquor, like all the advertisements and pictures glamourize.

I doubled down on my decision that I would be fine to drink as long as it was in moderation. However, the problem in my, oh so obvious, sound logic was that my definition of moderation is vastly different than that of a normal drinker.

One day, after working up to the nineteen-mile marker long run, I decided to test my theory. I stopped by the liquor store and picked up a half-pint of vodka; after all, clear liquors have fewer calories, and the last thing I wanted to do was start gaining weight back. Clearly, my priorities were straight.

I set off to just drink half of the bottle but ended up downing the whole thing. Instantly, my brain rejoiced, and I felt alive. My brain celebrated like the squirrel from the kids' movie *Ice Age* after he gets his fidgety little paws on an acorn. Just like Scrat the squirrel and his acorn, every time my brain would obtain alcohol, disaster was never far behind.

Within about eight minutes, the alcohol penetrated my brain and elated my soul. I felt great, and that was the scary part. I didn't feel guilty or dismayed at the fact that I had just reintroduced a major problem back into my life. I knew I couldn't tell Leigh-Ann, because she would just "overreact"; after all, she was only loving, supportive, brilliant, and more empathetic than any human I have ever met. I couldn't dare expect her to be on the higher plane of thinking that my dumbass was on.

After getting home, I realized that I was more buzzed than I wanted to be, and I didn't want Leigh-Ann to know. I decided that it would be best for me to go inside and take a shower, tell her that the run took a lot out of me, and I just needed to take a nap. After sleeping the buzz off, I woke up to her none the wiser. I flirted with the idea that I would be able to keep this up until I could convince her that I was ready to be reintroduced to "mature drinking".

Over the following month and the weeks leading up to the marathon, I continued to run with new vigor. I negotiated with myself that I would only drink after strong runs. This plan quickly led to me finding honorable mentions with every single run. I would have an easy, smooth stride, negotiate hill work well, maintain a faster than anticipated pace or finish strong in a sprint. No matter what small achievement I awarded myself, the trophy was always the same: a few shots of vodka. I convinced myself that since my running didn't seem to be suffering and Leigh-Ann didn't have any intimation that I was drinking again,

I must have been drinking a normal amount, even though I hid every drop I consumed.

As my race day approached, I looked back at my training and glowed with pride. I had lost a total of around forty-five pounds and had completed multiple organized 5ks, 10ks and half-marathons. I was finally drinking like a sophisticated gentleman; well, I was in my mind at least.

I'm not one hundred percent sure when it happened; I think it was after reading an article regarding what happens to your body during a marathon, but my brain zeroed in on the anticipation of the pain I was about to experience. My mind quickly burst into a brilliant display of anxiety and angst.

I am sure by now you have enough understanding of my personality to guess what happened next… that's correct; my friend and hype-man, the brain, whispered to me, "Hey, buddy, I bet since you have your drinking under control, you can probably take some of the lower end Percocet's without any issue."

I quickly responded, "I bet you're right!"

I reasoned with myself, *after all, if I broke my leg, I wouldn't expect myself not to take pain management.*

Two days before my big race, I found myself scoring twelve Percocet without much thought. I looked at them the same way one would look at a celebratory cigar. I didn't take them right away like I would have done months ago, which further fueled my belief that my addiction was cured. My suspicions seemed to be correct: all I needed was a little time away and a reset of my use.

I decided that I would carry all the pills on me during my race. My initial intent was to only take them after I crossed the finish line. As per usual, I would find my plan crumbling in my hands.

As I prepared everything for race morning, I worried that I would take all the pills just to ease my pre-race anxieties before crossing the start line. With that being said, my astute critical thinking kicked in and I thought to myself, *Why don't you take some alcohol with you to help ease the anxiety during your run? After all, you will be running so much, the alcohol should burn off before it has the chance to affect you.*

I know, I know, genius.

So, of course, my next step was to fill the water bottle that I would be carrying on the course halfway with vodka and the other half with an orange electrolyte sports drink. After all, I wasn't a fool, I wanted to make sure I stayed hydrated.

I set everything out the night before my race and planned to wake up at two a.m. Disney races, especially the marathon, have a reputation for being massive, so an early arrival isn't really a suggestion but a must. I knew that sleep was going to be sparse, so I decided the obvious course of action was to down a half-pint of vodka before laying down to go to sleep.

At two a.m. I woke up in a daze. I got dressed and headed off to the race. The drive took about forty-five minutes, and the parking was atrocious, albeit managing to be magically efficient, as most aspects of Disney are.

Exiting my car was very difficult, because it was so cold and windy. The temperatures were somewhere in the twenties, and for someone who has always lived in Florida, this was blisteringly cold. It never dawned on me that I needed to pack a throw-away hoodie or any other warm clothing. I wrapped myself in a trash bag that I had requested from a race volunteer. After wrapping myself in my makeshift windbreaker, I wandered aimlessly around the staging area until it was time for us to be ushered to the starting line.

I… WAS… freezing!

I stood behind a tent tie-down, trying to block the gnawing winds from infiltrating my bones. I was only able to find minimal relief. I vacated my insufficient covering in search of more adequate shelter. I found the perfect shelter inside a Porta Potty, where I sat for about an hour until the loud voice came over the speakers. I know what most of you are thinking, but I promise there were plenty of Porta Potties onsite, and me taking up refuge in this one wasn't keeping anyone from being able to use the restroom.

The announcers began directing all runners to the start line. I exited the dank refuge and found my place in line.

After about a half-mile walk, the cattle drive of runners made it to the starting line. Due to its massive size of around fifteen thousand plus runners, the participants were placed in different corrals based on expected finishing times, with "A" corral housing the elite runners. I found myself mid-pack, standing in the "L" corral. After enduring a crowded thirty-minute wait time, the race countdown began.

The starting line exploded in a spectacular firework display as the elite runners charged forward, like lions trying to outrun each other for the prized zebra.

It took about twenty minutes for my corral to finally approach the starting line. I stared down the dark course in bewilderment. I felt so grossly out of place, but there was no backing down now. Moments before the gun went off for our corral to launch, I steadied my nerves by taking a couple of swigs of my vodka-rich water bottle that I had prepped the night before. The taste of the alcohol calmed my mind as I focused on the task at hand.

The first six miles flew by as the sun started to rise. I was maintaining a strong pace and feeling good. My nerves started to rise up, and I convinced myself that if I could get ahead of the pain that I was about to feel, I may be able to maintain my strong pace.

I decided to take pre-emptive measures against the anticipated pain and broke out three of my Percocet's. I threw them into my mouth and quickly chewed them into a thick, bitter paste. I washed them down with my orange sports drink Screwdriver and continued to push forward.

A mile or two later, the pills started to kick in. The familiar numbness washed over me, and my brain erupted in a burst of euphoria. I quickly became very emotional about my running. I was so proud of myself and how far I'd come. Here I was, running a marathon and managing my drinking and pill use like a real classy fella.

It never ceases to amaze me how deluded a person in the grip of addiction can be.

After arriving at the halfway point, I started to notice that my legs were feeling tight. Now, instead of just accepting leg fatigue as a by-product of running a half-marathon, my brain reasoned that since I was feeling pain, the first three pills that I had taken surely must have burned off. This was a cause for celebration, because I could now take my next three Percocet's without the feeling of guilt.

Yet again, I know… solid logic.

For some reason, the next six to eight miles were a little hazy. I would love to be able to give a descriptive account of that section of the race, but for the life of me, I barely remember running it. I do however remember mile twenty distinctly. I remember thinking, *Man, I am at the twenty-mile marker, and this is where everyone says I should hit the wall. This really doesn't seem too bad, but to be safe I should probably take my next round of preparedness.*

Just like with my first two checkpoints, I chewed up three pills and washed them down with nearly the rest of the contents in my water bottle. I knew I was running strong because of my time; I was on track for a sub-four-and-a-half-hour marathon finish. Miles twenty through twenty-five were just as hazy as the previous set of miles. As I approached the twenty-five-mile marker, I knew I was going to do it. I was going to finish the Walt Disney World Marathon. I looked forward to seeing the twenty-six-mile marker, which is where I planned to do my victory dance. The only difference between my victory dance and another's is that mine didn't consist of an awkward jig, mine was finishing off the remaining pills.

True to form, at mile twenty-six, I could see the home stretch and the finish line. I remember Disney characters in costume cheering on the runners and thought now would be a good time to finish off my arsenal. I finished the remaining pills and the contents of my water bottle. I threw the bottle in the trash and popped some gum in my mouth, because I knew Leigh-Ann, Hannah and my mom would be waiting for me at the finish line.

As I approached the finish line, I wish that I could say I was overwhelmed with pride, but I felt mostly numb. Entering the last one hundred yards of the run, I noticed Leigh-Ann holding Hannah, with my mom standing next to them, screaming their heads off in support. I crossed the finish line and seconds later had a volunteer place a gold Mickey medal with a red ribbon around my neck. I walked a few more feet and another volunteer wrapped me in a metallic space blanket. I stopped to take my official finisher's photo before walking over to meet my family. Leigh-Ann and Hannah grabbed me and hugged me as tight as they could. Leigh-Ann told me how incredibly proud she was of me.

I tried to focus on her words, but it felt like we were in a tunnel, and she was getting further and further away from me. Looking around, I realized I was lost in a sea of people and quickly started becoming paranoid and claustrophobic. Just as we started to push our way through the crowd towards the exits, my recently ingested stomach contents pushed their way to their exit. I felt everything in my gut quickly making its way back up my oesophagus in a caustic rush.

I quickly scrambled to the side lines, where the perfectly manicured Disney foliage was. As I stepped up to the fencing, my gastric contents broke into the light of day. I sprayed vomit all over the beautiful horticulture. The perfectly groomed Disney Garden looked as if it were the set in a scene from *The Exorcist*. The fifty or so people that were around me vacated my immediate vicinity. I clearly remember hearing one guy say, "That's how you give a full effort and leave everything on the course."

Mortified, I quickly left the area before Leigh-Ann and my mom could smell the alcohol. A volunteer handed me a cup of water and I was able to rinse my mouth out and pop in some fresh gum.

I stumbled and limped to our vehicle, where I quickly reclined the passenger seat and promptly passed out. I woke up at home, crawled to my bed and slept for the following eight hours. When I woke up, I ate some food and felt better. I never gave a second thought to my drug and alcohol use on that day.

The one thing that was confirmed in my mind was that if I

was able to run a marathon while popping pills and drinking, I could not have as much of a problem as I thought I had. I decided that as long as I stayed off of the needle, I should be able to enjoy my vices.

As usual, this moron was wrong again.

Part 3

First Place to Rock Bottom

I once read somewhere, "Sometimes it takes an overwhelming breakdown to have an undeniable breakthrough."

Looking back to this time of my life, this statement speaks to my heart. I placed myself back on my kamikaze track without skipping a beat. I was in an all-out sprint towards a brick wall.

For the following year after my "spectacular" marathon finish, I continued to drink and pop pills daily. For the most part, I was convinced that since I was no longer shooting up, I no longer had a problem. My running continued to progress forward while I fell further and further behind in life. I completely used my running to affirm that I didn't have any substance issues. I would arrogantly think thoughts like:

Could someone with a drug problem really run a marathon?

AND

My metabolism is so high, I bet the drinks and pills aren't even having an effect on my physical health.

My rationale of thinking was completely warped by what I wanted to believe.

I continued to become sneakier and sneakier with my drinking and pill use. I tried so hard to keep Leigh-Ann from catching wind. I would hide liquor bottles of all sizes around the house. I would tape pint bottles of rum to the pipes under my bathroom sink. I would hide pills in DVD cases and in the pockets of never-worn dust-covered jackets that hung in our closet year-round. I had a half gallon of whiskey hidden in the mulch bag on the back of my lawn mower. I buried my treasures around my house like a drunk pirate.

I diverted all my attention to not overdoing it and appearing inebriated. The last thing I wanted Leigh-Ann knowing was that I had relapsed and was making strides back to my old ways.

Reflecting on this time, I cringe at the fact that my arrogance convinced me to believe that I was outsmarting everyone around me. I knew Leigh-Ann had her suspicions, but whenever she would bring up concern, I would play the role of a victim, who did not have any trust. She knew I was unwell; all the warning signs were there, but with me being totally shut down to discussion she was unable to voice her concern.

Throughout that year I completed multiple half-marathons and dozens of shorter distance runs. While my running performance seemed to get stronger and stronger, my mental health was still declining.

I steadily picked up more and more overtime until I was right back where I was before my in-home detox. I continued to expose myself to some of the worst that humanity has to offer. There was one call during this period that seems to stick out in my mind as another pivotal moment in my mental health digression.

This was the call that made me believe that PTSD was a real thing and not just a made-up disorder for people looking for attention. Unfortunately, back then this was a common mindset for first responders.

It was about one a.m., and my partner and I were on our way back to that station after dropping a patient off at the

157

hospital. It had been an exhausting shift and we were just praying that we could get some sleep. We made it about halfway to the station when my dispatcher's voice came over our radio.

"Medic 35, Medic 35, need you Code 2, for a welfare check."

My partner and I glanced at each other and threw our hands up in the air, followed by some select expletives. We were being sent to check on someone who had called 911 and said they needed an ambulance, then hung up the phone after requesting that we not use any lights or sirens in order to not disturb the neighbors.

Sounds like a real life or death emergency, I sarcastically thought.

Upon reaching the neighborhood, we informed our dispatcher that we were on scene and asked if there were any updates available. She replied, "Negative."

After a couple of choicier angry expletives, I keyed the radio back up and asked if the scene was safe for us to approach. She replied, in a snarky tone that this particular dispatcher was known for at 1 a.m., "As far as we know, and we have no indication to think otherwise."

I replied, "Copy," before slamming my radio on the dashboard.

My partner and I looked at each other and evaluated the beautiful and massive home that we were sitting in front of. This house was located in one of the most prominent sides of the city and could easily be valued at over a million dollars. We decided, both through complacency and sheer exhaustion, that we would investigate further without requesting back-up.

We approached the massive double front door, rang the

doorbell and knocked aggressively. After repeating the knock a couple of times, the door slowly opened and we found a despondent older gentleman standing in the foyer. He peeked his head out of the door and looked both ways, as if he were checking to see if any nosey neighbors were watching us. He quietly ushered us into his house as we asked him what was going on.

He walked us a few feet inside as he spoke erratically, while avoiding and ignoring all of our initial questions.

At first, I thought he was intoxicated or having some type of psychiatric issue, with the erratic statements he was making while avoiding eye contact. As he continued to try to walk us further into the house, my partner and I started to feel completely uncomfortable with the situation and stopped moving forward, as the red flags in our gut and heads started to wave.

After a few more steps, he realized we were no longer following him. We were slowly making our way back to the front door. As he turned around, I could see a mixture of anger and fear in his eyes as tears were streaming down his face. He made two or three more mismanaged statements before his entire face fell blank as he stopped talking and began to just stare at us. His attitude abruptly shifted as he told us, "Get the FUCK out of my house!"

At this point, the red flags in our minds were at full mast and waving frantically. Before we could even turn to make our exit, which was now about ten feet away from us, he reached into his robe pocket, pulled out a pistol and shot himself in the head right in front of us.

The room burst into a thick cloud of red moisture as the

sound of the gun bounced off the wood paneled walls and ricocheted deep into our chest cavities. My partner and I both took off in an all-out sprint out of the house within a fraction of a second. The scent of blood and gunpowder still lingered in the distance.

After making it to the safety of the front yard, I smashed the panic button on my radio, which sent out an SOS to my dispatchers and anyone else on that radio channel. I quickly keyed up my radio and gave a quick account of what happened, while we made our way into the ambulance to retreat up the street. Within minutes, the once peaceful neighborhood was now overwhelmingly flooded with police cars and fire EMS back-up. The rest of that night was a blur of recounting and reliving that moment while giving police and supervisors detailed accounts of what took place.

I wasn't even sure how to process what had just happened. I wasn't sure what I should feel or what I was even allowed to feel. All I knew was that I felt like I needed a drink.

I called Leigh-Ann, and as soon as I heard her voice, I broke down. I told her what had just happened, and I could hear the impact of what I had experienced through her shaken voice. I told her that I was done with this shift and that I was coming home. She agreed and said that she would be up when I arrived.

On my way home, I decided that I didn't care about keeping my drinking hidden any more. My mind sternly demanded that with what I had just been through, I deserved a drink, and Leigh-Ann would just have to deal. I took a pint of whiskey out of the glovebox in my car and cracked it open. By the time I arrived home it was already halfway gone. I walked into my house, pint bottle in hand, and I was met at the door by a shocked and concerned wife.

I think she was equally concerned about the alcohol in my hand and the events of the night. As I made my way into the house, I looked at Leigh-Ann and said, "I don't fucking care anymore," in an exasperated tone that dared her to question me.

She knew at that moment that this was not an argument that she was equipped to win and shifted her concern to the trauma that I had just survived. After showering and allowing enough time for the alcohol to completely soak in, I lay down to get some sleep without even discussing the call.

Waking up the next morning, I went straight for the liquor again. Leigh-Ann tried to intervene and redirect my attention to talk about what happened, but I told her, "Don't even try, I am fine. I don't want to talk about it, and I am going to have a few drinks to take the edge off until I can get past this."

Again, sensing the indignancy in my voice, she knew it was a losing battle. She bit her tongue and watched helplessly as I downed the liquor as if it were my job. I maintained this stubborn-headed, shutdown and indignant attitude for the next two months, while openly drinking and popping pills. Any time Leigh-Ann would bring up concern, I would hit her with the "I don't care" attitude.

As the months passed by, the Christmas holiday quickly approached. I lived life in a drunken blur. I don't remember much in this time because I was drinking to black-out any time I wasn't at work. Leigh-Ann and I argued intensely almost every day. If we weren't arguing, we were giving each other the silent treatment. She was at a complete loss and disadvantage with me. I victimized myself and framed the concern she had for my addiction as apathy towards the trauma I had been through. Looking back, nothing could have been further from the truth.

How do you fight fiercely for someone when the person you

have to fight is them?

She tried so hard, with pleas of love and negotiation to get my attention. It wasn't until the day after Christmas that I realized that I couldn't possibly sink any lower. I blacked out drunk on Christmas, ruining the day for both my wife and daughter. I was a drunken, mean maniac who broke dishes out of frustration in an angry tantrum because Leigh-Ann told me that I needed to "take it easy, for Hannah's sake".

I woke up the next morning, with the aftermath of a belly that had been filled with a cinnamon whiskey the day before. I was puking violently as my stomach contents emptied through my mouth and nose with force. I sat on the bathroom floor, hugging the toilet bowl. I was sober and unsure of how I got there. As I stared into the porcelain throne, I knew that this was bad. I could not remember any events from Christmas the day before. I could only vaguely remember breaking dishes out of anger and ruining the day. I knew I needed help.

Just as those thoughts pushed their way into the front of my brain, the bathroom door slowly opened. My wife walked in and shut the door behind her. She had her arms crossed and was staring at me softly through a gaze that suggested, I am so pissed off at you. I know you're hurting deeply, and I still love you so much, BUT PISSED NONETHELESS. She calmly sat at the edge of the tub as the whiskey-scented snot dripped from my face.

She didn't even need to say a single word. I broke the silence first, and all I could say was, "I know."

She replied, "I don't think you do. I can't continue to live like this anymore. I love you so much, and you are my entire world, but your drinking is out of control, and I can't continue to keep Hannah and myself in this situation if you are unwilling to get real help."

There it was… the final straw on this broken camel's back. I knew at that moment that I could finally put down the shovel, because I was at rock bottom, and the worst part was that I wasn't alone. I had dragged this amazingly beautiful, innocent soul with me. I had been in some very low places over the years – hell, only a year and a half earlier I was laying on this very bathroom floor after trying to kill myself, but I had never been this low before. I had no problem losing myself, but the thought of losing Leigh-Ann and Hannah was more than I could bear. I knew losing them would be worse than a thousand deaths. I felt my frozen, icy heart shatter into a pile of shards inside my chest.

I didn't even try to apologize or negotiate; I knew there was nothing I could say to make this better. I knew my words held no credit with Leigh-Ann. I was a master at making empty promises and over the years I had perfected my trade.

I told her that I loved her more than anything else in the world and that I needed help and I couldn't do this on my own.

I think I took her by surprise with my immediate willingness and lack of excuses. I knew I would never change until I took ownership of the mess I had created through the choices that I knew were wrong.

The moment I told her that I needed help, her face softened as the tears began to roll down her cheeks uncontrollably. I told her that I had tried this on my own and I had failed. I promised that if she would just give me one more chance, I would do things right. I would talk to doctors, therapists, look into programs, attend A.A. or whatever else it took to get me clean. I was always dead set against asking for professional help due to the stigma in my field.

None of that mattered any more. I promised that if she would find it in her heart to stick by me one more time, I would spend the rest of our lives making it up.

This time would be different. I always wondered how far I would fall before I felt that I was at rock bottom. The thought of Leigh-Ann and Hannah walking away from me was a rocky abyss that I couldn't fathom. With one very real threat from Leigh-Ann, my entire outlook changed.

This time I had to change, no matter how far I had to push myself.

Reader Rescue: I could write an entire book series on all the empty promises I made and strategies I tried while trying to quit drinking. I went through many detoxes during this time in my life, some easier than others, with my sobriety times ranging from a couple of days to a few weeks. I have detoxed at home as well as being under medical care and supervision. I am convinced detoxing is one of the most physically and emotionally crippling events one can go through and withstand.

There are many types of help and different pathways to success when it comes to overcoming substance abuse. It is a highly individualized process that should be approached as such. My best advice is to figure out the safest and best path for the individual. The best way to start the help process is to first consult with your medical provider.

The patient mentioned above in the horrific scene turned out to have a terminal illness and was looking for an out that he could control. It is common for people to commit suicide after calling 911, so that their families are not the ones that find them.

Chapter Nine

Part 1

Pressing Forward

"God, grant me the serenity to accept the things I cannot change, courage to change the things I can, and the wisdom to know the difference."

- Reinhold Niebuhr

It has been said that the only way to find heaven is by slowly backing away from hell. While I agree with this sentiment, I must respectfully disagree with this statement. I believe that the only way to truly find and appreciate heaven is to push yourself through hell until your breakthrough presents itself.

After my sobering ultimatum was handed to me, I realized just how far into the lake of fire I had drifted. I found myself treading in the deepest section, trying to keep my head from going under. My choices were clear: I could accept the final lifeline Leigh-Ann was throwing me or I could allow my depression, anxiety, anger and addiction to drag me down to the crushing depths, where I would most certainly meet my demise, likely at my own hand.

I decided to stand firm on my promise. I cleaned myself up and immediately called for professional assistance. I made appointments to meet with my primary care physician and found a therapist who was accepting new patients. It would be a few days before I could get in to see them, so in the interim I looked up the A.A. helpline and made my first call. This was one of the hardest calls I have ever made in my life; the phone felt as if it weighed five hundred pounds.

My call was answered by an empathetic and understanding voice. I hesitatingly explained why I was calling and asked how to get started. He congratulated me on taking the first and most difficult step: admitting I had a problem and realizing my life had become unmanageable. He went on to tell me that he was also an alcoholic and addict but had been sober for many years. I felt uncomfortably comfortable opening up to a complete stranger about one of the most humiliating struggles in my life.

However, once I started, I found it extremely easy to speak openly about my issues, especially after finding out that he had a very personal understanding as well. We ended up speaking for hours, as if we were old friends reuniting over tragedy. I could tell he felt the pain in my voice as he echoed back his own struggle, which in turn brought me comfort.

He searched my area in his database and found multiple options for me to attend an A.A. meeting. He provided me with a list of local places and times where other alcoholics met and supported one another. Lastly, he provided one piece of advice that resonated in my soul before hanging up. He told me that the only way I would ever get clean and enjoy life again was to be brutally honest with myself. As scary as that thought was, I decided that if I was going to do this, I would give it my best shot.

To say I was sceptical would be the understatement of the century, but after seeing how hopeful Leigh-Ann was that A.A.

could help me, what choice did I have? I started to entertain the fact that maybe my dumbass did not know everything. The only thing I undoubtedly KNEW was that what I was doing was not working. So, I decided to give a meeting a try.

What was the worst that could happen, I leave exactly the same?

After agreeing to attend a meeting that night, I decided to have a sit-down with Leigh-Ann and start my declaration of brutal honesty. I told her that I had been drinking since before my Disney marathon. To my arrogant surprise she said she knew. She told me that I wasn't as smooth as I thought I was, and she could tell every time I decided to drink.

She started crying and told me that she knew she couldn't confront me because of my explosive frailty. She opened up and said watching me kill myself over the years has been the hardest set of events that she had ever witnessed.

She told me that I slowly tortured her through the way I treated myself. My heart was broken at the thought of all the pain I had put her through.

I admitted that I hid alcohol and drugs all around the house. Before I could finish, she started naming my hiding places. She told me that she knew about the alcohol taped to the pipes, the bottles in the jacket pockets in our closet and a few others that I'd even forgotten about. I was so embarrassed that she knew everything the whole time. She was unable to do anything but patiently waited and hoped I would come to my senses.

We went around the house and gathered up all the hidden goodies that I had stashed. One by one we emptied them down the sink drain. It was cleansing for both of us. I watched the frustration take form by the aggressive way Leigh-Ann threw away the now empty bottles. At that moment I noticed just how much she hated alcohol. I felt the guilt continue to swell inside.

That night, I attended my first A.A. meeting. Strangely, I felt right at home. I decided to mainly shut my mouth and pay attention. Me thinking that I knew everything was what got me into this mess. I learned that I couldn't trust my brain to make good decisions, so I would look to people who had been successful at getting and staying clean. I decided that I would give my one hundred percent undivided attention to my sobriety. I knew if I wasn't unwavering that I would lose the two people who meant more to me than anything else in this God-forsaken world.

As directed by my new friends in A.A., I attended at least one meeting every day for the first ninety days of my sobriety. Some days I even attended two or three. I took an extended leave from work so that I could focus on myself during this time.

To be transparent, I knew my time as a paramedic was coming to an end. I had been messing up at work for a while and ended up on my department's radar. I was calling off from a ton of shifts and not performing my best while on duty.

Over the previous year, I slowly lost my good standing with my company. As quickly as I had built up my prestigious reputation, I watched it fall apart right before my eyes. I made the mistake and built my castle of shifting sands.

The truth is, I knew I needed to really sit down and ask myself if this was what I wanted to do with the rest of my life. I knew I wouldn't be able to successfully achieve sobriety this early while still focusing on other people's trauma and emergency. I figured it would be hard to lay a solid foundation during an earthquake.

I was doing extremely well in my recovery and started to earn back a quality of life. I worked the twelve steps of A.A. while continuously searching out new areas of my life that needed work. I bettered my communication with my family and found that I was a lot slower to anger. Overall, I was starting to see glimpses of my old life.

When the time finally came for me to return to work, I decided that I no longer wanted to run 911 calls. This was not a decision that was made easily or quickly, nor was it a decision that I intended to be permanent. While I could feel my mental and emotional well-being strengthening, I knew that I was too new to my sobriety infancy to be able to hit the ground running.

I was torn when it came to making this decision and I felt weak, as if I were running away from my issues. In hindsight, making this decision took more courage and strength than I realized at the time.

When I think back to it, I feel like it would have been an unrealistic expectation to have expected myself to maintain my sobriety in that type of atmosphere. Not that it can't be done: individuals most certainly can and do achieve this on a routine basis, but all I knew was that my heart was not in the right place, and it still harbored misdirected bitterness toward the 911 system. It wasn't fair to myself or my potential patients to enter back into the field with anything less than a dedicated heart.

I decided to take a job at a leading hospital within my city. My new position working in the emergency department was very laidback and redundant. I spent my days interacting with patients without the crippling weight of sole responsibility for their well-being. I looked at my time in my hospital position as my cocoon period. I felt safely nestled inside a shell of mediocrity and redundancy, but just like a caterpillar to a butterfly, this stage was not meant to be permanent, instead used as a metamorphosis to blossom into something beautiful.

After almost two years of a steady emergency department job and steadfast sobriety, I found myself experiencing the feelings of a rebirth. During these two years, Leigh-Ann and I strengthened our marriage and reinforced the love that we always had between each other. I continued to run on a recreational basis with the distant hopes of completing another marathon, but this time the right way.

Just like my running, my life and career seemed to be directionless. It's not that we weren't doing well in this stage; I just felt as if I had hit a point of stagnation. I felt as if there was no more room for me to grow; after all, the caterpillar can't stay in the cocoon forever.

I started to respect the person that I had become. The hard work and dedication I had put into my family and sobriety was very fulfilling in and of itself.

The problem was that there was something missing in my life. I had no idea what it was, but I knew something was missing. This missing piece created a small hole in my soul and kept me from feeling complete.

The chaotic puzzle of my life had slowly been put together piece-by-piece with order and care. The fact that there was still a single unknown piece missing from the center of my being was infuriating beyond words.

On my quest to find this missing piece, Leigh-Ann and I decided that it would be best for me to leave the emergency field altogether, in a quest to find myself. This was a huge leap of faith into the unknown, but I knew with Leigh-Ann by my side, her love and support would provide more than an adequate parachute.

Over the next six months, I worked odd-end jobs to keep the bills paid. I used this time to focus on myself. I had two questions on my mind and two questions only.

What am I passionate about, and what do I want to do with the rest of my life?

My sporadic running schedule started to firm up, because my time in my running shoes helped calm my mind and bring me clarity. I realized that the two things I was extremely passionate about were wanting to help people and wanting to turn all the negatives in my life that I had fought through into positives.

I started searching online using "Substance Abuse", "Mental Health", "Firefighting/EMS", "Jobs" and "Employment" as my key words. It must have been written in the stars or a part of some divine plan, but I happened across a company that was partnering with the International Association of Fire Fighters (IAFF), Firefighters Union. They planned on opening a substance abuse and mental health facility specifically and exclusively for firefighters, paramedics, EMT's and dispatchers.

The position was looking for someone with experience in the fire/EMS field and who was comfortable building an intake department that would be the first point of contact for any fire/EMS personnel seeking help.

Basically, I would be talking to my brothers and sisters in the field and helping to bring them ease at one of the most challenging points in their lives.

I couldn't think of a better suited job for me, even if I was able to construct it from scratch. I immediately sent my resume and waited in anticipation for contact.

Roughly after a week, I received a voicemail from the Vice President of Admissions for the substance abuse program that the Firefighter Union was partnering with. The voicemail expressed his interest in setting up a time and date for an interview. I tried to "play it cool" by waiting for about an hour before calling him back, but I am sure my voice couldn't disguise the giddy excitement I harbored at the prospect of such a perfect position.

The following week, I found myself in a suit and tie in the waiting area of the admissions facility.

After about a ten-minute wait, the Vice President approached with a smile on his face and hand extended. I stood to greet him, shaking his hand before being ushered back to his office.

My first impressions of him were very strong. He had a stern business deposition but a softness in his eyes that suggested that he truly cared about his organization and their mission to help people out of the grips of substance abuse. After exchanging the typical interview pleasantries and introduction questions, the questioning became a lot more personal.

On paper, he could tell that I would be a fine fit for the position, but keeping in his mission to make sure that I was the right person for the job, he asked me one simple question.

"Why do you think you would make a good fit as the spearhead of the firefighters admission department?"

At that moment, all hopes of playing it cool and providing professional and clinical answers went out the window. I could feel tears welling up in my eyes and that annoying tickle behind my nose that is indicative of an emotional response. I tried to gather myself before my tears rolled down my face, but before I could make any strides of composure, my eyes yelled, "Bombs away!"

I felt the warm tear roll off my cheek and strike my shirt as I calmly and briefly summed up the journey that led me to sit in his office on that day.

As I spoke as honestly and open as I could, I noticed his already welcoming demeanor soften even further. I told him that my only goal in my professional life was to help people. I went on to tell him that I couldn't think of any greater privilege than to work directly with my struggling brothers and sisters. I knew if given the opportunity I could turn the stumbling blocks that had tripped me up for so many years into stepping stones for others.

Who better to talk to fire and EMS workers about the struggles of their job than someone who knew what was like to be on that end of the phone? I told him that we as a demographic were very closed off people. I knew I could speak the language of someone struggling with 911-induced PTSD, depression, anxiety and substance abuse.

Being a compassionate person himself, he sensed the burning desire I held to help this very special group.

We ended the interview and he escorted me back to the front door. I thanked him profusely for his time and consideration. He reciprocated the gratitude for my interest and drive to join his team. He told me that he would be making his decision shortly and would reach out with his verdict.

After roughly three days, I received the phone call that I was so hoping for.

I HAD THE POSITION and they wanted me to start in two weeks. I graciously accepted without hesitation. The two weeks leading up to my start date were busy with all the pre-employment festivities, such as background checks, drug screens and mountains of paperwork from HR.

After starting my new position and acclimating to the office life, I quickly realized that I was working for a great company. The VP of admissions ran a well-oiled machine and took a great deal of pride in cultivating the company's culture. I worked with some amazing people, most of whom were in recovery themselves.

I started two months before the firefighters facility opened to receive their first patient. I was on the ground-breaking team that worked hard over the next year to create and nurture a relatable and compassionate intake department for our emergency responder clients.

As I write these pages, I can say that I was and still am a part of something very special. I can honestly say that everyone who has been hand-selected to work with our patients truly and sincerely wants the very best for them.

Fast-forwarding a year and a half into my new career, I was flourishing. We made it through all the growing pains that a new medical facility can expect and started making huge strides. I was in the best place professionally that I had ever been in. I found confidence in the fact that I was in the perfect position, with ample room to grow as both an employee and a person.

With my home life completely mended and thriving and my professional life glowing with promise, you would think that I had found that pesky missing puzzle piece. Unfortunately for me, that gaping hole remained open. I knew that this hole could not be filled by outward sources from my family or career. This was much more personal.

I came to terms with the fact that this hole was created by me as an individual. I had worked hard at accepting the things in my life that I could not change. I knew I could never go back in time and shield myself from the trauma and stress that I had introduced in such large quantities. I could, however, figure out how to use them to my advantage. I came to the realization that I could use my substance abuse, PTSD and suicidality in my favor, which gave me the confidence to attempt to mend this noticeable hole.

I had been motivated to do many things in my life to this point, but I was never more motivated than when I realized that filling this hole would bring wholeness to my life.

Part 2

~~Motivation~~
Drive

It was the summer of 2018. My wife and I took our daughter and my mother on summer vacation to the beach. This was the first vacation we had been on in years and my first ever sober. We spent an entire week lying on the sandy beaches and lounging poolside, soaking up all the vitamin D we could.

My daughter absolutely loves the beach and was filled with the energy that could only be found in a happy eight-year-old. She kept us on our toes, switching back and forth between the beach and the pool. She was having so much fun and it filled my heart to know that I was able to enjoy these moments without chemical-induced pseudo-relaxation.

After continuing the routine of making trips to the beach and back to the pool all morning and devouring a heavy lunch, I was ready to retreat to our darkened, cool hotel room to catch a power nap. Afterall, we were on vacation.

As I lay in the soft linens, I jumped on YouTube to venture down a rabbit hole until I fell asleep. I watched a few recommended running videos which triggered the YouTube algorithm to recommend more videos of the same content. After about three to four bland videos, the following recommendation caught my eye.

"The most motivational talk ever – David Goggins –

Driven".

I noticed that the video was over thirty minutes long and was sceptical that I would finish. I played it anyway in preparation to drift off to sleep. Surprisingly, I could have never prepared for the impact this video would have on me.

The video was an "Impact Theory" interview of the former Navy SEAL and all around badass, David Goggins. From the moment he started speaking, I was all ears. He spoke about his horrible childhood and challenges that he faced growing up, including bullying and exclusion. He touched on the fact that as an adult, he felt directionless in life.

In rough summary, one night after finishing his shift as an exterminator, he arrived home with a milkshake and bag of donuts and turned on the TV. He said he turned on the Discovery Channel and started watching a documentary about "Hell Week" in Navy SEALs training.

Goggins described the feelings he had watching the recruits getting their asses handed to them, as he was a two hundred and ninety-seven-pound man who was unhappy with his life. He then took a long, hard look at himself and realized just how depressed he was. He decided to implement change at that moment. He made a very powerful statement that stirred my heart.

"The only way I was going to find myself was by putting myself through the hardest and worst things possible."

David went on to declare that he was on a mission to callous his mind for whatever life decided to throw at him.

At this point of the video, we were a mere four minutes in, and he had my full undivided attention. I sat up in the bed and focused on his every statement. He spoke with so much conviction, honesty and passion that he commanded attention.

177

As he continued to tell his story, he talked about quitting his job the very next day after watching the Navy SEALs documentary. He had met that stagnation point that I had felt working in the emergency department.

David decided that he was going to become a SEAL, even though he was scoffed at by most recruiters. It took him about three months to lose around one hundred pounds in order to be accepted to Navy SEAL school. After being accepted and arriving at the training facility, he would have his ass handed to him over and over. He ended up repeating and enduring through "Hell Week" three times due to medical issues that kept knocking him down.

Instead of giving up, he continued to press forward with whatever the instructors threw at him. He developed the ideology of "taking souls", where he refused to show any sign of weakness to anything or anybody who was trying to break him. He graphically described the injuries and mental turmoil he endured during the training and discussed the pride he felt at his graduation as he became a Navy SEAL.

The Host of "Impact Theory", Tom Bilyeu, then made the statement, "I find it interesting that we as a human species run from pain. I firmly believe that you need something that is brutal, is difficult and is hardship, that will knock you off-center and makes you feel bad, because in the process of clawing back, then you can become something. Unless you've tested yourself and put yourself through the ringer, you have no hope. The only way to grow is to suffer."

The thought struck me like lightning.

I knew what it was like to be a powerless victim of my circumstance and fight my way back. I now needed to know what it was like to selectively choose to enter into struggle with the confidence that I was no longer a victim but an overcomer. I needed to take extreme ownership of my shortcomings and use them as fuel to push me through an elective hardship.

David went on to say that one of the secrets to his success was learning to be "very comfortable with being uncomfortable."

Was this it?

Was this the missing piece of my puzzle?

My soul jumped at the opportunity to prove myself and fight to earn my respect back in its entirety. My only problem was that I couldn't just up and join the Navy like Goggins did. I needed to figure out something that I was able to train towards while holding a career and being a full-time dad and husband. It had to be something that would bring me to my knees, kick me in the teeth and set me ablaze, before allowing me to emerge from the ashes.

At this point in the video, I was standing up, pacing around my hotel room. I felt my soul stirring and new life washing over me. I felt excitement. This was a feeling that I had missed for many years, a feeling that I had almost forgotten.

As I continued to listen to Goggins, he arrived at the point of his story where he described that he missed the struggle of SEAL training. He made a promise to himself after graduation that he would always expose himself to things that made him uncomfortable and challenged him. One thing he stated that he always hated and was never good at was running. On his quest to callous his mind, he knew that he needed to lace up his running shoes.

After deciding to use running as a way to raise money for recent fallen SEALs, he decided to look up the hardest foot race in the world, The Badwater 135, a one hundred and thirty-five-mile race across Death Valley in the middle of July. Temperatures typically hover around one hundred and twenty to one hundred and thirty degrees Fahrenheit for the duration of the race. David was intrigued and decided to call the race director for entrance.

Chris Kostman, the race director of this incredible race, told him that he needed to qualify for participation. He wasn't able to gain access based on his merit as a SEAL alone. Chris recommended a twenty-four-hour race in San Diego the following week and told him that if he could run one hundred miles in twenty-four hours, he would consider him for his race.

As one to not back down from a challenge, David signed up and less than a week later found himself standing at the starting line.

David went into even greater illustration of this race. He talked about how he kept up with a world-renowned women's champion for the first fifty miles, before she started to pull away.

He went on to describe in very graphic detail his self-implosion around mile seventy. He stated that he was "pissing blood down his legs" and on the verge of delusions. He made the mistake of sitting down in a fold-out chair, where he proceeded to "shit up his back". He was forced to continue sitting there, because his blood pressure was so unstable that every time he tried to stand, he felt like he was on the verge of blackout.

In the interview, David told the host that he learned during the last thirty miles of this race, "A human is not so human anymore."

He made the claim that he didn't know if he would be able to continue. He decided to attempt to stand up and slowly walk to the portable restroom to get himself cleaned up. He said that when he stood up, the pain that he felt was excruciating. He described it as the worst pain he had ever been in, and coming from Goggins, that says a lot. It was during those instant waves of pain that he realized that the last thirty miles of this race were a life-changing moment for him. He described them as the hardest thing he had ever done and felt that he was on the "brink of death".

He decided his only plan of attack was to cut the last thirty miles into manageable sections. He then said, "Motivation is crap. Motivation comes and goes. When you're driven, anything in front of you will get destroyed."

After he cleaned himself up, he began shuffling his feet. His wife accompanied him back onto the one-mile loop course and started to pace him. He limped to mile eighty-one, where his wife told him that he wasn't going to make the time – he was walking thirty plus-minute miles.

Upon hearing the devastating news, he looked deep within himself and made up his mind that he was going to take this race's soul. He immediately started running and continued to run the last nineteen miles of the race non-stop.

After crossing the finish line as a broken man, he went home, where his wife had to basically carry him up their stairs and lay him in the shower. He was still urinating blood and unable to control his bowels. His wife wanted him to go to the hospital, but he just wanted to enjoy that moment. He had placed himself in the struggle and overcome it. Later that year, he found himself at the finish line of the Badwater 135.

As I write this section, I still have no idea why something so painful and crippling sounded like something I wanted to attempt. Most people DO NOT want to lose control of their bowels. I, however, was intrigued.

I finished off the video in complete awe. Again, I knew I couldn't go out and join the military, but for the life of me, I was having a hard time thinking of an excuse for not attempting a one-hundred-mile run.

Before that video, I would have bet my entire salary that it was physically impossible to travel one hundred consecutive non-stop miles by foot.

After a quick search for "one hundred-mile races", I learned that there is an entire subculture of amazingly extreme "everyday people" called "ultramarathoners". I thought to myself, *if I can complete a one-hundred-mile foot race, there's nothing I can't do!*

I reasoned with myself that if David could do it, so could I.

The idea immediately took root and spread throughout my spirit. I felt the excitement continue to grow as I narrowed my Google research to "one hundred-mile races in Florida". Within a couple seconds, I was staring at the KEYS 100 website, a one-hundred-mile foot race from Key Largo to Key West, Florida. The race website described it as, "Spectacular! This southernmost part of the United States is a chain of islands surrounded by the turquoise waters of the Atlantic Ocean and Florida Bay/Gulf of Mexico. Picturesque and laidback, the scene is a sub-tropical paradise".

The race promised to challenge runners through some of the most beautiful tropical scenery in the United States. I looked up the race date and celebrated when I found out it was the following May, eleven months away. I figured that this would give me plenty of time to train and wrap my brain around this seemingly impossible feat.

I was ALL IN, without a second thought. I had no idea

what I was getting myself into, but I was IN nonetheless.

I refused to continue to live my life timidly, afraid of relapsing or becoming overly stressed then relapsing. I was driven to change the things in my life that I could.

Part 3

Wisdom to Know

After a few minutes of gassing myself up in the dark hotel room, I decided to share my newfound goal with my family. I wanted to tell them my intentions and create some accountability. I walked out onto our balcony and saw them sitting poolside. My daughter was jumping in and out of the pool, perfecting her dives. My wife and mother were sitting under an umbrella, talking away.

I briskly walked down the stairs to join them. As I approached, I locked eyes with my wife. She could tell I was walking towards them with a purpose. Once I made it tableside, my wife confusedly asked if I was able to get some sleep. I took a seat and just blurted out, "So, I've decided that I'm going to run one hundred miles."

The confusion on my wife's face increased as my mother's face joined in.

"What?" my wife replied.

"I'm going to run one hundred miles… I just watched a motivational video that talked about running one hundred-mile races in a single effort and… I want to do that," I replied in a proud voice that was backed by zero confidence.

Both my wife and mother let a humorous and expected scoff escape before further questioning me.

"What do you mean, run one hundred miles straight?" my

wife asked.

Before she had even completed her question, my mom interrupted, "Is that even possible? Can people do that?"

They both stared at me in predictable disbelief, and I could tell that they had no idea where this was even coming from. I realized that the last thing I had told my wife was that I was heading up to the room to catch a nap after tiring myself out by eating a huge lunch.

Then, after about forty minutes, I came rushing down the stairs, insisting that I was going to run one hundred miles. It's no wonder they were confused.

I slowed the conversation down in an effort to connect the dots and further explained the interview of David Goggins. I explained to them that I felt a desire to place myself in a struggle to prove to myself that I was capable of overcoming.

After hearing that explanation, the chuckling stopped, but the disbelief stood firm. As I continued to uncontrollably provide a steady stream of word vomit, I felt as if I left my body and watched the interaction from a third-person perspective. I watched as a chubby, out-of-shape man tried to fumble his way through an explanation of why he wanted to run so ridiculously far.

I continued to watch as he nervously chattered on and on about urinating blood, "pooping up his back" and pushing himself to the point where death seemed to be a sweet relief. He babbled about blisters, stress fractures and shin splints like a pre-teen girl describing her favorite boy band.

Instantly, I was sucked back into my body, staring at my wife and mom as they looked like deer stuck in headlights. My wife was left utterly speechless as my mom asked, "What… in… the… hell… are you thinking?"

I sincerely responded, "Come on, mom, you have to admit, it sounds like a little bit of fun."

The shock and confusion had grown to a critical point and a meltdown was imminent. I'm sure their first internal thought was, *did he relapse?* which I think was a fair suspicion, given the magnitude and suddenness of such a lofty goal.

I continued to fill the uncomfortable silence with Lord knows what, while I watched the confusion in my wife's eyes morph into fear.

Even though I am sure she was just saying it to pacify me, Leigh-Ann let out a final exacerbated chuckle while making the declaration, "If that is what you want to do."

Also, I'm sure she was only being agreeable in hopes that within a few weeks this conversation would be a distant memory, one that I would look back on and cringe while having a good laugh. Over the last couple of years, I had been anything but consistent with my exercise. Every now and then I would catch a whim and run two to three miles a couple times a week. These short spurts of "weekend warrior mentality" were not exactly a stable foundation to build the confidence it took to tell people that I was going to run one hundred miles in a single effort.

Little did anyone know that my one-hundred-mile declaration was ironclad in my soul. I'm not sure if I even truly believed I could achieve this, but my heart told me that I had to try.

After I ran out of steam during our conversation, I just sat there awkwardly in silence while my wife and mom processed all the information that was dumped on them. The silence became deafening, until I awkwardly segued the conversation by asking, "So, what's for dinner? All-you-can-eat Chinese buffet?"

As our vacation ended, the days turned to weeks and the weeks to months as I obsessively talked about everything running. When we arrived home from the beach, I wasted no time starting my training while soaking up every piece of running information I could find. I downloaded books, read blogs, listened to podcasts, consumed magazines, and watched as many YouTube videos as I could.

After about a month and a half of solid dedication and obsessive, compulsive running, my wife saw that I was taking this one-hundred-mile vow seriously. The familiar fear and worry resonated back in her eyes.

The day finally came when I was ready to seal the deal and make a financial investment towards my goal. I approached Leigh-Ann and told her that I wanted to sign up, pay my entrance fee and reserve my spot at the starting line of the 2019 KEYS 100.

After nervously telling Leigh-Ann that it was time to sign up and explaining that this was just something I had to do, she reacted in the one manner that I wasn't expecting.

Leigh-Ann told me that this was a huge undertaking and that she legitimately worried about my health. She further explained that it was going to be very hard on her to watch me break myself, and she hated to think about me being in that level of pain. After voicing all her concerns, she ended the conversation in the most amazing way. She said she believed that if anybody could do it… it would be me.

I've always, throughout our entire life, been the one underdog Leigh-Ann would bet on.

I don't know where her faith in me came from; I guess it doesn't really matter. The fact was I now had her blessing to move forward with this goal. Within about fifteen minutes, I was reading a confirmation receipt for the iconic KEYS 100 ultramarathon.

Having enough faith and confidence in myself to sign up for this race was a pivotal point in my recovery. It was the first time since getting sober that I didn't feel meek and timid. I felt confident and in charge of the course of my life. After hitting that submission button, I knew, for better or worse, my life wouldn't be the same.

Since becoming sober I would pray, "God grant me the serenity to accept the things I cannot change, courage to change the things I can, and the wisdom to know the difference."

I now had the courage to change the course of my life and the wisdom to know it could be done. Now I just needed the belief that I could accomplish it.

Chapter Ten

Part 1

Road to Ultra

"If you want to run an extraordinary distance then you must put in an extraordinary effort."

- Michael D'Aulerio

I was all in and there was no backing down from this one. I made a declaration to myself, to my wife and basically to anyone who would listen to me gab on about running. I had invested finances towards the KEYS 100 and now it was time to let the rubber sole meet the road.

I started firming up my running consistency during the month and a half that I first learned about one hundred-mile races and actually signing up. I now had roughly nine months to complete my training and preparation for my adventure. This was quite literally the gestational period of my running; I would nurture and attend to it while it grew and developed. I took great care during this period, in hopes that my first one hundred-miler would turn out to be my rebirth.

I learned very quickly that running every day on the same route was not as easy as it sounds. Monotony has a strange way of creeping in and making any repetitive thing you do increasingly difficult. Due to my extremely demanding work schedule and my desire to keep my running from having any significant impact on family time, I was forced to complete almost all of my training on routes near my house.

Instead of dwelling on how insidious the monotony was, I decided to attempt to use it to enhance my runs. I thought back to what Goggins said about "callousing your mind", and I realized that if I could transform my runs from a strictly physical workout to a physical AND mental workout, I would reap double the benefits.

I pushed myself and refocused my mind to use my runs as a meditative and reflective time. I taught myself how to capture my thoughts and take control of them before they had a chance to focus on the negatives. Learning to do this wasn't only a game changer to my runs but also to every other aspect of my life.

Throughout my journey to sobriety, over the last few years, I tried many different approaches and strategies to help maintain the gift of sobriety. I took part in programs, talked to multiple doctors, saw therapists and even tried medication briefly. All these steps were very impactful in their own way and, depending on the person, can be the missing piece to their puzzle. For me, however, the therapeutic benefits that running provided were by far the most beneficial modality that I ever ran across... pun intended.

There is something special to be found in setting goals, especially lofty ones, and executing steps towards their completion. I would be hard pressed to find any point in time in my life where I was more driven and prouder of myself based on a personal goal.

I was amazed at just how far my self-esteem was raised after one decision. I couldn't believe that after years of hovering over and finally kissing rock bottom, I would get to a place where I started to actually believe that I may be able to achieve the "impossible" and in doing so learn that I have no limits.

While my running was coming along strongly and quickly, my mental health seemed to be sprinting miles in front of it. My runs became an intricate part of my recovery during this time period.

Every week, Monday through Friday, I would arrive home from work, lace up my tennis shoes and report for my therapy session. My therapist was hardened and relentless in her search to find the truth within me. There was nothing that I could get past her, and she was able to look deep into my soul.

If I had a bad day or I was stressing about something, she knew. If I wasn't eating right, sleeping well, or treating myself as I should, she knew. She was always there, day and night. Through blazing sun and pounding rain, she continued to call for me.

While most people refer to her as the road, for me, I called her doctor.

She took me through ups and downs that most people would call "hills". For me, however, the ups and downs were exposure therapy for the peaks and valleys of my life. She was in a constant search for the best in me and would demand that I give nothing less than my finest. She built me up and helped me believe in myself once again.

During the following months, my training became more effortless. This is not to say that it became easy, but I found a joy in it that helped change my perception.

My only aim during training was to focus on myself and

what I considered progress. I stopped paying attention to my times and stopped comparing my runs to what others considered to be "good". My running was a time for me to recalibrate myself from the stresses of day-to-day life, not to impress people on social media. It seemed that the less I cared about my pace, the faster I was completing my runs. As I got stronger, both physically and mentally, my runs became longer. As my training developed and strengthened, I searched out new opportunities to get the most benefit and inspiration during each and every session.

I chose to download ultrarunning audiobooks to listen to on my longer runs. It truly fanned the flames of my momentum, to derive inspiration from some of the greats of the sport. I devoured books such as *Can't Hurt Me* by David Goggins, which went into much further depth of his journey, *Ultramarathon Man* by Dean Karnazes, which a lot of people consider to be the ultramarathon bible, *Nowhere Near First* by Corey Reese, *Reborn on the Run* by Catra Corbett, *North* and *Eat and Run* by Scott Jurek, *Running Man* by Charlie Engle, and all three books by the late David Clark, may he run in peace.

Some of the most inspiring thoughts that I have ever had came from the pages of these awe-inspiring people. I chose to saturate my mind with stories and memoirs of people who found their peace by pounding the trails before me.

As I learned to deal with the monotony of my runs, I noticed my brain no longer would put up a fight, and it stopped complaining when it was time to hit the road. I quite literally ran it into submission.

As with most feral things learning to be controlled, I also had to offer it some positive reinforcement. As a reward for its compliance, I elected to reward it with organized races. I decided to start signing up for some longer-distance races that I could utilize as training runs. I signed up for a handful of marathons and a 50k, to take place about four months before the KEYS 100.

I was excited to dip my toes back into the racing scene and wondered what it was going to be like to cross a marathon finish line sober and clear-minded. I was looking forward to enjoying a race the right way.

I learned over my few months of training to prioritize my happiness and mental health over pace, time splits and expected finish times. Not that these things are not important or useful tools, but for me it was more about fueling my race on my happiness and joy of being out there. The only expectation that I held myself to was giving it my absolute best and never giving up.

Five and a half months into my training, I found myself standing at the start line of the 2018 Space Coast Marathon. It was an out-of-this-world space exploration-themed race that I highly recommend to anyone looking to run a fun and well-organized 26.2 or 13.1-mile race. I was excited, nervous and sober. My mind was racing long before the starting gun went off.

As I stood among the sea of people in the launch corral, I was overwhelmed by emotion. I found myself getting teary-eyed at the thought of the emotional race that I had run to make it to this point. I wondered where I would have been if Leigh Ann had never had that difficult conversation with me.

Before I could fall into that black hole of nightmares, I realized the stark and morbid truth. If I was honest with myself, I would have probably been dead or in jail.

I quickly stopped myself from dwelling on the what-ifs and refocused on the task at hand. I had become exponentially good at taking my thoughts captive before they got out of hand and incited an emotional and physical response. I focused on the race director as she announced the runners' welcome and the racecourse expectations for the day.

After a few moments of loudspeaker encouragement, the sea of people shouted in unison as we counted backwards, "Three... two... one!"

Instead of a race gun going off, the Space Coast Marathon utilized the "Project Mercury" rocket blast off.

If one finds the sharp bang of a starting line gun motivating, listening to the rocket's bellowing blast through all the speakers and subwoofers is nothing short of exhilarating, and just like "Project Mercury", we were off.

Within a few minutes of crossing the starting line, my nerves departed like rocket boosters as I reached my orbit. I fell into a smooth and comfortable stride as I pushed myself through the first six and a half miles of the race.

The course took place through a beautiful residential neighborhood bordering the waterway's edge. I vividly remember what it was like to watch the sunrise over the water. I was so thankful for how far I had come, not in the race, but in life.

After the first quarter of the race was behind me, I buckled into my already comfortable stride and prepared to ride it out for the long-term. As the miles flew by, I began to feel my body start to get tired. This was expected and welcomed. After all, what's the point of a marathon if it's not difficult?

Somewhere in between mile eighteen and nineteen, I was finally able to truly experience every real marathoner's rite of passage. I was running smack dab in the middle of my wall. While this part of the race truly sucked, I couldn't help but feel happy that I was experiencing this. Overcoming this obstacle was what made a marathoner's achievement worth bragging about. I thought back to the hundreds of pages of content that I had ingested over the last five months regarding navigating "the wall".

I slowed my pace down a bit, focused on my breathing, ate a couple of gels, drank some water and then continued to push through. Around mile twenty-two, I hit my breakthrough. My mind and body collaborated in digging in deep and pushed me through. I found myself falling back into my smooth and easy stride as I soared to the finish line.

As I approached the final half mile of the race, I prepared to cross the finish line. I was nothing short of elated with my performance of the day. I knew after crossing this finish line that I would have actually earned the title "marathoner", and I would have the pain of leg and back cramps to back up my claim.

Crossing the finish was an amazing moment. A smiling volunteer placed a beautiful medal around my neck and wrapped my shoulders in an official Space Coast Marathon finisher's beach towel. Leigh-Ann, Hannah and my mom were standing near the side lines, cheering and taking pictures.

As I approached my family, I pretended like I was going to vomit into the bushes as my wife's eyes became large with concern. Once she realized I was making a joking reference to the Disney fiasco, she gave me a stern, sarcastic "that's not funny" glance before cracking a smile. She wrapped her arms around my neck and told me how proud she was of me and my daughter was holding a large poster board that read "Dad, you are my hero" on one side and "Dad, did you poop your pants?" on the other.

It was exactly the type of cheering I needed. It put a huge smile on my face and a laugh in my heart. I was so incredibly thankful to have them present. I took my time savoring the moment and taking it all in.

After crossing the finish line and making it to our vehicle, I felt relatively strong and well. I knew that this was a training run in the grand scheme of it all and looked forward to my next event.

My next event would be my introduction into the ultramarathon world. I signed up and planned to run the Clearwater Running Festival 50k in January.

This would be a beautiful thirty-one-mile run on the pristine Gulf Coast of Florida. It advertised beautiful Gulf beach views, complete with clear waters, sun and sand. I had about two months to convince myself that running an extra five miles would be "fun".

I planned to step up to the 50k distance in an attempt to dip my toe into the ultra-community. Little did I know I would saturate my entire self with it.

Part 2

Soaked and Stoked

After completing the Space Coast Marathon, I took a couple of days off to recover and relish in my victory. Once I was able to successfully lower and lift myself from the toilet without the customary struggle of a marathoner, I jumped right back into training as the Christmas holiday came and passed the following month.

As I wrapped my mind around taking the next step of my journey of becoming an ultra-athlete, race day came faster than a speeding train. Once again, I found myself standing at a starting line, completely overwhelmed with feelings. However, this time there was one drastic difference.

The feelings I was consumed with were not of the emotional kind but more of the physical. The 50k that advertised sunny beaches and pristine water looked more like a scene out of the movie *Forrest Gump*, when Lieutenant Dan was sitting in the crow's nest, screaming at the hurricane.

It was around twenty degrees Fahrenheit with a torrential downpour.

As I stood in the freezing cold weather, soaked to the marrow, I looked down at my feet and noticed that where I was standing had about three inches of water collecting on the road. The only way the starting line could have been wetter was if they had placed it in the nearby ocean.

Everyone was huddled close and bouncing up and down in an attempt to stay warm as we continued to wait for the starting gun to go off.

As soon as the countdown was over, all the brave souls who had decided to show up set voyage to the race of their chosen distances. For me it was thirty-one miles on roadways that resembled flowing rivers.

I told myself, as I ran, that the weather would break, and warmth would come with the sunrise. Keeping in nature with Florida weather, the light presence of rain that was forecast for that day was, as usual, grossly mis-predicted.

After completing mile six with absolutely no change to the downpour and no sign of a sunrise through the blackened and gray skies, I gave up on the hopes of reprieve and came to terms with the fact that this current situation was my life now and would be for the next five to six hours.

I accepted the fact that I was unable to change the weather and knew that the only variable that I was able to change was my mindset. I decided to use this terrible weather to thicken the callous pads I was developing on my mind. I told myself that if a little bit of rain was the worst thing that happened during this run, I would be happy.

Around mile ten, the continuous cold and drenching rain started to finally take its toll on me. I felt like I was losing body heat at an alarming rate. Every layer that I was dressed in was soaked. The only time my feet were not completely submerged in water was when they were being lifted out of it to run the next step. As I write these pages, it is still the coldest I have ever felt. Again, keep in mind I was born and have lived my entire life in the subtropics of Florida.

I have to give a huge shoutout and kudos to all the runners

who live in truly cold climates and still force themselves to get out in the blistering cold.

Approaching the 13.1-mile marker, I took notice of the sign that directed the half-marathoners to exit the roadway at this point. I caught myself fantasizing about taking the exit and ending my race early. I thought about how nice it would be to have Leigh-Ann come pick me up and take me back to the local hotel, where I could jump in a hot shower.

The moment I realized that this creeping thought was expanding in my brain, I quickly took it captive and discarded it. While it was insanely impressive for anyone to complete any race distance in this God-awful weather, my mission was far from over.

I had come here to achieve the title "ultramarathoner", and come hell or higher water, I wasn't walking away without it.

I knew I had to get past this point of the race as quickly as I could, so I reached down deep and busted out a sprint pace to put as much distance as I could between me and the safety of the 13.1-mile rip cord. I know this isn't the wisest pace strategy at this point in someone's first 50k, but desperate times call for desperate measures.

After putting about a mile between me and the early finish, I backed off of my pace and tried to reclaim my lungs. I slowed my breathing back down and placed myself back into a stride that was sustainable.

One nice aspect about busting out a sprint is that it gave me a tiny bit of body heat back. However, this bonus was short-lived.

I was able to talk myself out of not veering off at the 13.1 exit, but my running drive would be tested yet again at mile marker 14.5. As I approached the aid station at that mile marker, I saw the volunteers dividing the marathoners from the 50k-ers.

They were signaling the marathoners to turn right and directing the 50k runners to continue running straight through to the five mile out-and-back turn around. This section would need to be completed before coming back to rejoin the marathoners' course.

My brain congratulated me for not ending my race at 13.1 miles, and as a reward it gave me permission to drop down to the marathon distance. After all, in this weather that would still be very respectable.

I did agree that while completing the marathon in this weather was beyond respectable, I had to remind my brain that this was not my mission. Again, it was going to take more than rain to stop me from becoming an ultramarathoner.

As the race volunteer asked me which distance I was running, I responded, "I am one of those 50k idiots."

He chuckled and informed me that most of the 50k runners had elected to drop down to the marathon distance and take the marathon exit.

I told him, "While that sounds great, I don't think I could be any more soaked or freezing, and I am already miserable, so what's another five miles?"

He gave me a quick look of admiration, pointed me down the 50k direction and told me, "Well then, go get it."

As I took off running, I responded back jokingly, "And get it I shall."

Exactly three steps down the five mile out-and-back, my brain lost it! It instantly went into a frenzy and tried to incite panic. If I could have recorded my internal dialog, I am sure that it would have gone something like this.

Hey, idiot, what exactly are we doing here?

You know we are probably going to die, right?

Hypothermia IS a real thing!

You are going to be the first fool to ever die of hypothermia in Florida!

That nice guy back there said that most of the other 50k runners decided to drop down to the marathon. Where the hell do you get off thinking you can do better than them?

I HATE THIS, I HATE THIS, I HATE THIS!

As my brain continued to scream at me, I realized that I had not eaten anything since the banana on my way to the race. I broke out my handy dandy gels and downed a couple of packages.

Within about ten minutes, my brain resembled a screaming infant that had just found their peace in a pacifier. Once my brain was subdued, I glided through that five mile out-and-back with ease.

When I approached the aid station, that kind-hearted volunteer was still under his umbrella, directing runners. He smiled as he saw me approach and directed me back on the course to finish the race.

As I passed him, he told me, "Only about ten miles left."

I nodded and thanked him for being out there as I confidently ran past with my chest out, chin up and a new, bolstered sense of confidence.

As my brain started to grumble and stir again, I downed another gel and quickly neutralized it from throwing another tantrum.

I thought to myself, *less than a half-marathon to go!*

I cranked up the gritty rap music in my headphones and

dug in once again.

The following three miles ran through a beautiful residential neighborhood of million-dollar homes directly on the waterway. It was easy to distract myself during this section by letting my mind wander and fantasize about one of the owners of these beautiful estates coming out, handing me the keys and telling me this home was now mine.

I always find it entertaining to see just how far your mind can wander while your body is in a running autopilot. Some of my most vivid and enjoyable daydreams stem from running.

After finally making it out of the neighborhood, I was back on the main strip of Clearwater and sailing towards the finish. I noticed another runner ahead of me maintaining roughly the same pace. I did what most other runners do and made him my focal point. I pictured him as a prized marlin that I was reeling in on these uncalm waters. I distracted myself by focusing on closing the distance between him and me.

Arriving at the 26.2-mile marker, I was standing shoulder-to-shoulder with him. I looked over and greeted him and complimented the weather. He chuckled and we had a good laugh together. We were both exhausted and freezing. Once we found out that we were both running the 50k, we quickly determined that we were not in each other's age group.

We decided that we were better off keeping each other company than we were running against one another.

We discussed the typical things runners talk about while suffering out miles together. We went into depth about why we chose to be out here in this terrible weather and what our overall hopes were with running in general. He was a great guy and I wish I could remember his name, but sadly my brain was frozen and gassed.

We navigated the last of the race together until we got to mile marker 29.5-ish. I then told him to go on without me. I wanted to get my mind in the right headspace and burn every little detail of the end of this race into my soul. I was about to become an ultramarathoner and wanted to give the accomplishment the sole attention it deserved.

I made a quick call to Leigh-Ann and told her I was crossing the last of the intercoastal bridges and should be crossing the finish line in about ten minutes. She and Hannah were sitting in the warm car, watching for me.

As I made that last climb over the steep bridge, the wind sliced through me like a knife. At the top of the bridges, the wind blew in strong and fierce gusts. I could see the finish line and nothing else seemed to matter. I no longer cared about the rain, wind, or freezing cold temperatures. I was about to achieve something I never thought possible of myself. I was about to officially become an "ultra" athlete. This title was earned and no matter what, no one could ever strip it from me.

I ran the final stretch of the race and crossed the finish line. I found the guy I had run with earlier, still standing there waiting to congratulate me. I shook his hand and thanked him for the conversation and entertainment. He reciprocated before heading off to his car.

After receiving my medal, I looked up to see Leigh-Ann and Hannah huddled under an umbrella, trying to stay dry. I trotted over to give them a hug and kiss before telling them that I wanted to find out my official time.

We headed over to the timing tent and provided the volunteer with my bib number. She glanced at her computer and looked up in excitement. She announced that I had won first place in my age group with an official time of 6:25:23.

At first, I thought it was a hypothermic delusion, but once Leigh-Ann repeated it back for confirmation, I knew I had heard right.

I won my age division!

At that moment, it didn't matter to me that most of my age group either dropped down to the marathon distance or didn't show up at all together. To be honest, that fact made the win even more sweet. I was so incredibly happy and proud of myself for sticking it out when every variable was stacked against me.

Although I was soaked to the bone and felt frozen solid, my heart was filled with warmth. I briefly celebrated with Leigh-Ann and Hannah before retreating to our car, where Leigh-Ann promptly blasted the heat to start the thawing process.

Sitting in that car seat, exhausted, while my whole body shivered was an amazing feeling. It was a discomfort that I had earned and celebrated in. I was not just soaked and stoked...

I WAS AN ULTRAMARATHONER!

Part 3

The Prodigal Run

2019 was off to a great start. I wore my new ultramarathoner badge with honor and found a deeper appreciation for the sport. I continued to run with purpose, focusing on form and time-on my feet, over distance. I knew that the KEYS 100 was quickly approaching and I was determined to be as prepared as I could.

I joined a Facebook group named FUR, Florida Ultra Runners, and was instantly inspired by so many men and women who were accomplishing amazing feats on the regular. I was also surprised at the amount of wisdom and encouragement I witnessed there. I made an introduction post discussing my goal to run the KEYS 100 and was met with an abundance of advice from people who had run it in the past. I was so thankful for this resource. These supportive people had me thinking about things I had never even considered. FUR is still one of the most encouraging and positive groups I'm involved in.

One piece of advice I received was to attempt a fifty-mile race before stepping up to a one hundred-miler.

Now, I know this should be common sense, but I never really gave a second thought to going directly from a 50k to a one hundred-miler. After explaining my plan to the runners in the group, I was met with cautious support. I was told that it was more of a mental benefit to take the step to a fifty-miler before leaping into triple digits.

They went on to explain that a fifty-miler would give me a mental edge going into the KEYS. There is a huge difference between running for six to seven hours versus running from sunrise to sunset. It would also give me a chance to really put all the strategies that I picked up over the past months to practical use. It would give me a chance to really figure out what worked and what didn't.

I discussed my new concerns with Leigh-Ann and asked what she thought about me attempting one final race before the KEYS. She had offered amazing support over the last few months and had backed all my decisions to financially invest into my one hundred-mile success, including signing up for multiple races. By the time we had this conversation at the end of February, I had already run multiple races and spent a ton of money on traveling and supplies.

Leigh-Ann hesitatingly asked which race I had in mind. Looking back, I probably should have had that figured out before pitching the idea. I laughingly said that I would have to circle back. I knew that I was asking for a lot: between time and expenses, running is no cheap sport. She saw the nervousness in my face and heard the hesitation in my voice, and she proceeded to calmly and supportively say, "Figure out what race you want to run, within reason, and we'll make it work."

I quickly jumped back onto Facebook and threw the idea out to my trusted "FURbies". Feedback was almost instant… the Everglades Ultras fifty-miler.

I was told by everyone who responded that this run was amazing. It was directed by the same race director who oversaw the KEYS 100: Bob Becker.

Bob is an incredibly decorated ultra-runner himself. He completed and set records at some of the most infamous and difficult races in the world, including running a double Badwater 135 at the age of seventy and the Sahara Desert-based, Marathon Des Sables. In addition to his impressive running history, I have yet to find one negative statement about him or his races. It seemed that everyone who ran any of his races raved about them.

This definitely had my attention. I decided that the Everglades fifty-mile race would be my last stop on the road to running one hundred miles. I told Leigh-Ann and she insisted that I sign up immediately.

The race took place in March, the following month. It gave me about three to four weeks to prepare. I was extremely excited about lacing up and hitting a trail instead of roads. I knew it was going to be a unique and memorable experience; I would soon come to find out that it would be one of the most healing events of my life. I had no idea at the time, but I was about to discover the puzzle piece for which I had been searching for so long. The piece that would bring me to wholeness and completion.

Race morning was an entirely new experience. The vibe at an ultramarathon is vastly different than marathons and shorter-distance races. In my experience, the ultrarunners are immensely more friendly and approachable. Everyone seemed to have such a laidback attitude in relation to the miles and struggle they were about to set off into. I, however, did my best to appear cool, calm and collected. I am sure if I were to look at myself from the outside in, I would resemble a duck sitting on water, appearing cool and calm on the surface while underneath the legs are paddling quickly.

I looked around at all the runners who surrounded me and for the first time in my life, I felt like I belonged on the starting line. I am not sure if it was all the smiling faces or the joking banter between runners who had obviously suffered through races together, or maybe it was due to the fact that I felt like I had earned the right to stand here, but for reasons unknown I felt at home.

I had been laser focused on my running and mental health during this entire journey. Standing at that starting line, I remember staring at the course and wondering what the day was going to bring.

As the race countdown came to an end, we were off. I had placed myself strategically in the back of the pack. One of the major goals and strategies that I planned on implementing at the KEYS 100 was to run based on how I felt and not allow myself to get swept up in the emotions that are common at starting lines.

As I slipped into a comfortable and conservative pace, I found myself running stride for stride with another man named David. We instinctively started to talk and found that we had a lot in common. This was his second year in a row at the Everglades 50, and I looked forward to any tips or tricks that he could provide on the fly. He was a really cool guy, and he offered a lot of information and good conversation as we started to tick off the miles.

David and I fell into a synchronized stride and pace. He informed me just how difficult this race could get and that I needed to save my energy. With his experience of this race in the past, I was more than happy to listen to him.

Running with a conservative pace allowed me to take in all the scenery. We found ourselves running in an enchantingly beautiful course. We were running down the soft dirt trail that could easily become muddy with the slightest rain. Luckily for us, the weather in south Florida leading up to the race was beautiful, and we had a soft but firm texture to run across, minus the hidden roots and knuckles.

On both sides of the trail there was a slight drop off that was filled with gorgeous emerald-green waters. The waters bubbled every thirty to forty feet, indicating a natural spring source.

On top of the water, much more frequent than the spring openings, were massive floating heads attached to what could best be described as dinosaurs that mother nature forgot to eradicate. I have lived in Florida my entire life and have seen thousands of alligators over that span, but never have I seen such massive freaks of nature as I did in the Florida Everglades.

Although the tram we were running on offered no real protection from the huge lizards, the path was remarkably peaceful to run on.

Exiting off the main trail to run the spurs was a fantastically unique experience. These paths were notably narrower and more technical. I couldn't help but feel like a real trail runner while carefully navigating these sections. As we continued to run down the canopy-lined trails, it felt like a scene out of a Florida-based *Jungle Book*.

As the miles continued to melt away, David and I found ourselves at mile twelve and still deep in conversation. It turned out this wasn't the only race I would be seeing him at; he was also planning to run the KEYS 100 in two months.

During the next twelve miles, we had the pleasure of catching up to and being passed by other runners. This allowed us to talk to and get to know some new faces along the run. This was an aspect that was completely foreign to me, having mainly focused on the marathon scene.

Now, I am not saying that there aren't personable or amazing people at marathons and shorter distances; I am just noting that in my experience, there is not much talking amongst runners during the race. This was an extremely refreshing change of pace… pun intended.

One thing I learned on this run is that there are truly resilient and amazing people in this world. It also seemed that everybody who was running the longer distances was also resilient in their personal lives.

It was strange to learn that everyone I spoke with had some sort of trauma or struggle in their life that they were in the process of overcoming. I spoke to men and women who wore their struggles on their sleeves and were comfortable sharing with a total stranger. This was a mark of strength that I profoundly respected.

I spoke to other addicts and alcoholics in recovery, along with people who had been through childhood trauma, sexual abuse, eating disorders and a wide array of other life-altering issues, including bankruptcies, loss of businesses and divorces. I was moved to tears at the discussion of some of the issues I heard. I felt a strange, yet deep, connection with everyone.

It was around mile twenty-four or twenty-five of the Everglades 50-mile Ultramarathon when I realized that I was not just here running this amazing course with other runners – I was out here navigating the trails of life with my tribe.

As I passed the halfway point, the notorious Florida heat was kicked into full effect. There is a level in the "old school" Nintendo *Mario Brothers* video game where the sun attacks and tries to kill you. I am almost certain that the creators of that iconic video game modeled that level after the intense Florida heat. Nonetheless, the race was still amazing.

Other than the marvelous course, impeccable direction of Bob Becker and the insane bragging rights one would earn after completing an accomplishment of this magnitude, another gem of this particular race was its selection of volunteers.

Every single aid station along this course was staffed with some of the most spirited volunteers that I have ever encountered to this day. Anyone who has ever ran a foot race knows that the volunteers can make or break a course.

The volunteers in the Everglades were a special type of special. Not only did their boisterous and cheerful demeanor distract from the soul-crushing despair of someone who has just run a gratuitous number of miles through a swamp at the hottest and most humid part of the day, but they were also incredibly efficient at their posts.

I remember one volunteer in particular: her name was Rachel. I would come to find out later that she was David's wife. I think she perfectly embodies what it means to be an ultra-volunteer.

I remember making it to her aid station in an all-out "death march". She could see me struggling from a distance and headed up the course to meet me. She complimented me on how strong I looked and how well I was doing, in a convincing way that distracted from the fact that it was a bold-faced lie. As I started to unfasten my sweat-saturated hydration vest, she pulled it off my shoulders, sweat and all, and asked what I needed.

My brain was semi-fried as I responded, "I just need a bathroom."

She pointed me in the direction of the Porta-Potties as she ran back to the aid station tent with my pack.

Making my way to the sewage-scented hotboxes, everything started to spin. The minute I set foot inside the blue outhouse, the increased heat and the smell of the breakfasts from all the runners ahead of me punched me in the gut. Instantaneously, I started to dry heave. It was a miserable few minutes as I finished my business.

The one silver lining was that upon exiting into the fresh air and lower ambient temperatures, the humid swamp felt refreshing by comparison.

I made my way to the aid station table as Rachel was making her way to me with a fully stocked pack. Not only did she have my pack's bladder full of ice water, but she also had the pockets of the vest stuffed with goodies that would provide some much-needed calories.

The extra hand-held water bottle I was carrying was also completely filled with an ice-cold electrolyte mix. She coached me to eat some pretzels as she filled the pockets running up the spine of my cooling skin shirt with ice.

After getting a handful of pretzels and some candy in my face, she lied to me once again, told me how strong I was looking and sent me off.

Once I was about a quarter mile away from that aid station I felt like a new man. I continued to scarf down more calories as I felt my strength replenish.

That was it: wall number one down.

I continued to implement a run and walk strategy that really seemed to be working for me. This is one of my favorite parts about the longer distance races: walk breaks are not only expected, but most of the time they are considered a smart and strong strategy. Fifty-mile races for the most part are an all-day event. If you are going to be in picturesque scenery all day you might as well enjoy it. One of my favorite sayings is, "Run your race fast enough to finish but slow enough to appreciate it." I was doing a good job of following those instructions.

Around mile thirty, I came to a short out-and-back spur. The direction was to run down it until I hit the turn around and then run back. It would equal roughly a three to four mile round trip.

Simple enough, right?

Wrong!

I'm not sure if it was because that section was notably more technical or if it was because by this point in the race my legs felt like I was wearing concrete shoes, but this little spur kicked my ass! The softer terrain of the trams I had been running on all day sapped the energy from me with precision, and at this point I was feeling each and every step I had taken throughout the day.

Every time I tried to get into a running grove, a tree root seemed to jump up and lasso my foot. More and more frequently I found myself face down on the trail. It became so frustrating it was almost comical... ALMOST!

I feel like I spent more time on my hands and knees bracing the impact of my stumble and fall than I did on my feet. I felt like a complete idiot, covered in dirt and mud, as the runners ahead of me approached on their return trip back to the main trail.

As I passed every one of them, we cheered each other on in a customary style of camaraderie. I noticed that almost every runner was covered in mud and dirt as well, some even bleeding from the palms and knees. I realized that I was not alone in my struggle to stay upright in this section.

I watched as one woman mis-stepped and ate the earth right

in front of me. When stopping to find out if she was okay, I found her laughing and crying at the same time. I gave her a hand up and discovered that she was not crying because of an injury but out of frustration. She looked me square in the eye and said, "Fuck... this... shit!"

I have never agreed with someone more in my life.

After finally making it to the turn-around point, I made a quick stop to take in the scenery. I noticed a huge gator sunning itself on a massive cypress log protruding from the bubbling water.

I jokingly thought to myself that if I waded into the water and instigated him to rip my leg off then I would have an excuse to not have to run back down this spur. Just as I chuckled to myself, I turned around to head back to the main trail and boom, just like that I was on my face yet again.

After letting out an exacerbated grunt and slamming my fists into the ground, I got back up and started high-stepping my way back up the trail. It only took two or three more falls before I declared to myself that this was idiocy. I decided that instead of continuing to risk injury to both my body and my pride, I would make better time if I just walked it all the way back... and that is exactly what I did.

After seeing a few more runners stumbling their way down the course, I finally made it back to the main tram. I had never been so happy to see a smooth-graded trail in my life. The race volunteers on the course pointed me in the right direction and off I went.

I was at mile thirty-one and still moving pretty good. I was headed towards another very challenging section of the race. The next section would take me out from under the safety of the canopied trail and into the wide-open sunny sky of the prairies.

This section was very uneven; it was created by all-terrain vehicles that had cleared out a small path through the knee- and waist-high grass. The prairies were a stark contrast from the lush green swamp that bordered it. It was as if we had stepped out of the Florida Everglades and stepped into the plains of Africa.

The heat and direct sunlight in this section was utterly demoralizing. The distance of this stretch is a little vague in my memory. I believe it was somewhere between ten and thirteen miles, and when I was done I would only have around six more miles left to the finish line. This is the only thought that kept me pushing through.

During the prairie section, I cannot remember seeing any other runner who actually looked strong. We all sort of fell into a synchronous death march. An outsider watching the events take place would probably have thought they were looking at a bunch of widespread prisoners heading towards the gallows with their heads hung low.

The only oasis from the heat and the overwhelming mileage was the three aid stations that you would visit. The central prairie aid station was a little slice of heaven that you would come across three times as you ran the different sections of the prairie.

The volunteer crew at this aid station consisted of Scott and Lisa Devona and their two sons. Scott and Lisa are a married ultra-endurance power-house couple, both bringing a well-decorated resume of experience to the table.

They were the exact type of pumped-up and experienced personalities that I needed in this stage of the race. Every time I entered their aid station, they seemed to know exactly what I needed even better than I did. Upon leaving their station all three times, I left with a much-needed boost of confidence and drive.

After finally completing my prairie stretch, I felt completely crushed as I headed into the final six miles of the race. I found myself all alone as I re-entered the swamp. My legs and back were cramping, and my mind seemed to be unraveling. It was hard for me to choose an emotion to cling to; I am certain I went through them all.

Finding myself in complete solitude, I had a chance to reflect on my life. I started to evaluate all the fullness in it, but I couldn't help but feel that the gaping hole was still there. I had no idea what it was going to take to make me feel complete.

I began to evaluate every aspect of my life, especially in all the areas that I had worked so hard to repair. Then it hit me. There was one area that I discarded that I knew needed to be addressed. With all the hell that I had been through over the years, I had pushed away the most important relationship in my life: my relationship with God.

The instant that thought filled my head, my heart started to excitedly motion to me as if we were playing a game of charades and I was getting close to the correct answer. I quieted my brain as I prepared to do something that I hadn't done in years. I was preparing myself to pray and truly mean it.

As my heart tore open and started to spill out a raging stream of emotions, my tear ducts followed suit. The feeling of peace that overcame me was indescribable. It was one of the most beautiful moments of my life. My heart, spirit, soul and mind came together as one and purged all the guilt and shame that I had been carrying from the moment I became sober.

It was during these three miles, in the middle of a swamp, that I rediscovered God, healed my faith, and finally became whole. For me, this was the most important piece of the puzzle;

without this final piece the rest seemed meaningless.

I felt an intense and rushing feeling of rejuvenation. I felt reborn. The heaviness and fatigue of the race and weight of the guilt and shame dissipated as my legs started to run with purpose and strength once again.

As I approached the forty-six-mile marker aid station, I noticed a bubbly, cheerful and familiar face. It was Rachel.

As I approached the aid station, she told me how strong I looked coming up the trail, and this time I knew she wasn't lying. She asked me if I needed anything and I responded, "No, I think I am fine. I would just like to top off my water bottle."

She smiled and happily obliged.

Before departing, she gave me a hug and words of encouragement, as she had done to the runners who came before me, and with that final "attaboy" I was off.

Still running strong, I was cruising towards the finish line. As the sun started to set, I realized that every person who had recommended the fifty-mile distance, and this race in particular, was absolutely right. This race was a once-in-a-lifetime experience that I would remember and cherish forever.

During my last mile, I was finally in range of cellular service, and I was able to call Leigh-Ann. She and Hannah were anxiously waiting at the finish line for me. I told her that I would be there momentarily and picked up my pace.

Turning the final corner of the race, I found myself staring at the finish line. I held my head high and smiled from ear to ear as I crossed and earned the bragging rights of a fifty-mile finisher.

A volunteer approached me and congratulated me on my finish. She placed a running alligator-shaped finisher's medal around my neck while a photographer was snapping pictures.

Leigh-Ann and Hannah quickly made their way to me with

217

extended arms. Leigh-Ann hugged me around my neck while Hannah sunk her face into my sweaty, soaking-wet shirt... that embrace did not last very long once they realized how grimy I was from running around a swamp all day.

I looked Leigh-Ann straight in the eyes and said, "I still have more in me; I'm feeling great!"

My declaration took her by surprise as she responded, "That's great, because in two months you'll run that distance twice."

It was a sobering thought.

After taking a few seconds to savor the moment, I made my way to the timing table to gather my official finishing time. The volunteer quickly told me that I had finished in 12h:42m:45s. He went on to exclaim that I had also come in first place in my age group.

Again, I found myself standing at a finish line in complete shock, and again, it did not matter to me that I was the only one in my age group that actually completed the race. This was the exact confidence boost that I needed.

I was now in the final stretch of my journey to the KEYS 100. I had not only completed my first 50k and fifty-miler, but I had also come in first place in my age group in both.

For me, it was an extraordinary outcome to an extraordinary effort. I had found a tribe that I could relate to and felt a sense of community that I had not experienced since I was a sober paramedic. I was happy with where I stood, both in the race results as well as in life. I knew what it was like to give running my everything. I would soon come to find out how it felt to have my running take everything.

Chapter Eleven

Part 1

Toeing the Line

"I learned that courage was not the absence of fear but the
triumph over it. The brave man is not he who does not feel
afraid but he who conquers that fear."

- Nelson Mandela

As race week for the KEYS 100 arrived, Leigh-Ann and I both
let out a sigh of relief. Not only had the moment finally arrived
that I had been patiently training and waiting for, but Leigh-
Ann, Hannah, my mother and I were planning to travel down to
the Keys for four days before race day in order to take in some
sun and enjoy some much-needed rest and relaxation before the
big day. It felt surreal to actually load down the rented minivan
and start off on the adventure we had planned so long for.

I was as prepared as someone could be heading into their
first one hundred-miler. I devoted HOURS to reading every
single article, blog, post and watching every YouTube video that
I could find about the KEYS 100. I made my family, who would
be acting as my crew members, watch crewing videos as we
discussed almost every aspect of the race and what everybody's
role would be.

Our drive was filled with nervous and anxious chatter that echoed all the months of training and preparations. By the time we entered the Keys, it was already about ten thirty at night. The weather was angry as we drove through a pouring rainstorm accompanied by a magnificent lightning show. The drive in was very eerie; the only light that was guiding us was the widespread dully lit red streetlights. The Florida coastline uses red lights near the water so as to not confuse the sea turtles. It felt like we were driving through a Stephen King novel.

As we drove to the halfway point of the KEYS 100 course, we finally arrived at our resort in Marathon. It was absolutely gorgeous. We quickly unloaded the van and settled into our rooms. We decided to call it an early night in order to wake up and take advantage of as much time as we could in the Keys.

The following three days were filled with snorkeling excursions, jet skiing, ocean swimming, lounging about and soaking in the unique and laidback culture of the Florida Keys. True to the description of the race, we found ourselves vacationing in paradise. The crystal-clear turquoise water was breath-taking. Everywhere you looked resembled a tropical paradise calendar.

Making it to Friday was a bittersweet checkpoint. On one hand, I couldn't wait to get the race events started, but on the other, I hated to see the vacation portion behind us.

Driving to the starting line, in Key Largo, was a much different experience than our drive to Marathon. The dark, eerie passages were now well-lit bridges carrying us over waterways that resembled an artist's palette of rich blues and stunning greens.

Pulling into the parking lot of the hotel that was hosting packet pick-up was an exhilarating feeling. We instantly recognized all the crewing vehicles. The crew vehicles were easy to distinguish, because they were covered in window paint and encouraging poster boards for the individual runners or relay teams. Upon exiting our van, I'm sure I looked like a kid anxiously coaxing his parents through the parking lot at Disney World to quickly get inside the park.

After entering the hotel and making our way to packet pick-up, I had the same sense of camaraderie that I had experienced in the Everglades. I was once again surrounded by my tribe.

After picking up my race goodies and bib, there was a mandatory orientation for all runners and crews. Bob Becker and an array of race officials sat as a panel and went over every aspect of the race. They were very thorough with all the information and answers they provided to both runners and their support. Bob especially warned us about two of the most infamous areas on the course: Hell's Tunnel and the Seven Mile Bridge.

Bob described Hell's Tunnel as just that, a tunnel through hell. It was a four-mile stretch of the course between mile marker forty-three and forty-seven, surrounded by marshy overgrowth with almost zero shade. When entering this section, runners can't help but notice that it is significantly hotter and more humid. For the most part, it is the section of the race that most runners dread.

The Seven Mile Bridge was also a challenge on its own. It was a seven-mile span between mile marker fifty-three and sixty. This section would force runners onto the shoulder of the road that was approximately five feet wide. Due to traffic being unable to stop on the bridge, this section would have to be navigated uncrewed. Race officials cautioned runners to stay as alert as possible, because there was nothing protecting you from the vehicles that would be flying past.

After sufficiently scaring us and telling us he would see us in the morning, Bob bid us goodnight and good luck.

As my crew and I headed back to Marathon, we stopped at an amazing local steakhouse and seafood restaurant. I am not sure if this meal was more of a celebratory dinner or if I felt the same way an inmate would feel on death row as they enjoyed their last meal.

Once we finished stuffing our faces, we made our way back to our resort in an attempt to get some much-needed sleep.

Sadly, sleep was not on the books for me.

After arriving at our room, all the last-minute preparations came rushing to my attention. My anxiety kicked into high gear, and I was instantly overwhelmed with all the little things I still needed to do. During what felt like a minor heart attack, I heard a little voice in my head saying, "Don't be a fool and overcomplicate this. Your only job tomorrow is to run."

I wrapped up my preparations and lay down to get some shut eye. Most runners have issues getting sleep the night before a big race. This was a vast understatement of what I experienced. As I lay wide awake, I played a game with myself called stare at the ceiling, then the wall and back again at the ceiling. I was fantastic at this game, and I earned a high score that night.

I obsessed over every detail of what tomorrow would bring, until my brain was finally too exhausted to stay awake. After closing my eyes and finally falling asleep, my alarms started sounding after what felt like four minutes. I jumped out of bed as if air raid sirens were going off.

Once I was finished getting ready, we loaded in our van and made our way back to Key Largo and to the starting line of the 2019 KEYS 100.

Upon arriving at the starting line, my nerves erupted into an all-out raging panic. I was no longer just anxious; I was now terrified.

My brain fabricated every single "what if" scenario it could piece together and shot them at me in rapid-fire fashion. I tried every technique I could to calm my nerves as I awaited my staggered start time. I realized quickly that there was nothing more I could do to calm my mind. The only course of action left was to show up in my starting corral and place my toe on the line. I had no control over the circumstances that the day would throw at me. All I knew was that I refused to let fear paralyze me in place.

As the race official counted down from ten, I took a few deep breaths and told myself that no matter what the day brought, I would face it with courage and adapt to the best of my abilities. With those final thoughts I took my first step past the starting line.

I am not sure if it was the adrenaline or if my dumbass just forgot to breathe, but I found myself struggling to catch my breath a quarter mile into the run. The moment my oxygen-deprived brain finally got my attention, I could already feel my heart beating at the same metronome as someone frantically sending an S.O.S. in morse code. As I drew in a deep breath of hot, humid and salty air, I thought to myself, *it is WAY too early in the run for me to feel like this! I need to SLOW myself down!*

I broke the number one cardinal rule of ultrarunning by starting out way too fast. It is common knowledge within the ultra-community that the number one commandment of long-distance running is, "Thou shalt not start off too fast."

Based on this first commandment, I was not just a heathen but a hypoxic one at that. I quickly adjusted my pace and focused all my attention on slowing my heart rate down and bringing in as much oxygen as I could. Within a couple of minutes, the spots I was seeing disappeared and the panic in my brain quieted down as well. I fell into a stride that seemed comfortable and sustainable.

After a few minutes of smooth running, it was time to take a mental inventory of how I was doing. Everything seemed to feel comfortable except for one blaring aspect: I was soaking wet and drenched with sweat.

I knew at that moment that I had majorly underestimated the heat and humidity in the Florida Keys. As I mentioned before, I was born in Central Florida and spent my entire life living in the sunshine state. As a native Floridian I can honestly admit that I have never felt heat and humidity that was even comparable to that of the KEYS 100. Within the first three miles of this race, I completely understood why this was one of the suggested races for the Badwater 135 application.

My original plan was to meet my crew every five miles for the first twenty miles of the race. I quickly called Leigh-Ann at around mile three and told her I needed to adjust the expectations. I asked her to meet me at mile four, because I was already in need of a refill for my empty hand-held water bottle and I needed to fill the three pockets that ran up the spine of my cooling skin shirt with ice. It was a sobering thought knowing that I was at mile four of this one hundred-mile trial and already feeling dehydrated and overheated.

After meeting with my crew at mile four, refilling my water

bottle, grabbing a bite to eat, packing my ice pockets with ice and hearing some much-needed sweet encouragement from Leigh-Ann, I was off.

As I started running down the course with the rest of the ultra-warriors, Leigh-Ann asked me how far she should go before they stopped to meet me again. I told her that I would call her in a few minutes to let her know, because it would depend on how quickly I would run out of fluid and how quickly my ice would melt.

It was about five minutes later that I called her, panicking and told her that I would need her to stop at every designated crew location that was pre-approved by race officials. Designated crewing stations were located every two miles or fewer. For further support, every ten miles there was a mandatory check-in and aid station, complete with volunteers and supplies.

By the time I had reached mile seven, my water bottle was bone dry again, as was my mouth. We continued the same routine of meeting, filling my water bottle and packing my shirt with ice every one to two miles.

After arriving at the mile ten check-in, I announced my bib number and continued to run through quickly. While the aid stations at this race were amazing with volunteers and supplies, I knew lingering would be detrimental to my pace. I made it a point to quickly push through as fast as possible.

After mile ten, I started to ease into the idea that I was going to be at this all day. While my brain pointed out how miserable I was, my spirit combated it by telling me how well I was doing. It was an internal conflict between two titans fighting for the alpha position.

Our strategy to meet every one to two miles was working out great. Not only did it provide me ample opportunities for hydration and nutrition but it provided me the most important fuel to my race — encouragement from my family.

By mile twenty, the sun was directly overhead and one important aspect of this race that I need to stress is its overall lack of shade. This course is infamous for its heat, humidity, sun and struggle... and boy, oh boy did I understand why. While the ice that was packed into my shirt at every crewing point was keeping me from succumbing to the heat, it unfortunately was causing problems of its own that I would not recognize until it was too late.

As the ice melted and cooled my body, the excess moisture ran down my legs and collected in my shoes. From about mile five, my shoes and socks stayed saturated. Obviously, this created an uncomfortable feeling, but little did I know how significant this issue actually was. When I stopped at my crew vehicle at mile twenty, I decided I needed to change my socks to a dry pair. It was after sloughing the drenched socks off my feet that I realized just how much I had messed up.

Part 2

Miles 20–40: Blisties

My feet were a mess! The water that had collected in my shoes, mixed with the hellacious heat, caused my feet to macerate. Both of my feet were pale-white and soggy to the touch. The deep wrinkles developed nooks and crannies along the soft bottoms of my feet.

My toes were developing blisters at an alarming rate. This was the first time in my life that I had ever developed a blister during a run. My socks already had traces of blood from the blisters that had popped themselves and oozed into my waterlogged sock. I was in complete shock when I saw the condition of my feet.

How could I run fifty miles through a swamp and not have a single foot problem, but twenty miles in the Keys made my feet look like soldiers' feet in Vietnam?

Leigh-Ann and my mother both looked at me with surprise in their eyes. I think they were both looking for reassurance that my feet were supposed to look like this. I looked right back at them with the same amount of surprise. Hannah finally broke the tension by interrupting the silent panic by saying, "Daddy, I'm so proud of you; you're my hero."

That was all I needed to hear. I filled my dry socks with

powder, in an attempt to draw some of the moisture out of my feet. I then slid them into my soaking-wet shoes. The cooling sensation of the menthol powder brought a short-lived reprieve as I topped off my water bottles, loaded myself down with ice, shoved some food into my mouth and headed off once again.

As I slowly walked away from the aid station, I turned around and saw my crew still watching me. Even with the distance between us, I could tell by the way they were standing that they were very worried about me. I tried to pull it together for their sake and started to trot until I could hit a slow running stride. Glancing back again I saw them loading into the van and preparing to drive off to the next aid crewing point. I knew what they were thinking; it was the same thing I was thinking.

How in the hell was I planning to run another eighty miles on these feet?

I quickly took that thought captive and disregarded it before I had a chance to really think about it. I recognized that my mind was wandering into sketchy waters with thoughts like that. It made no difference to my situation to dwell on all the things that were going wrong. My spirit knew the answer to the question anyways.

I would complete the next eighty miles by taking one step at a time. I didn't need to know how to run eighty miles; all I needed to know was how to run the next step. If I continued to only focus on the next step, the finish line would come to me.

I refocused my mind and distracted myself with the amazing views from the frequent and magnificent bridges. This was an attempt to keep my mind from drowning in a sea of negativity. I allowed the positive thoughts to stay and discarded the unproductive ones. The more I maintained a steady and consistent pace, the less my feet hurt.

As the miles gradually passed, I found myself steadily maintaining an ad hoc run–walk ratio. I would run when I could and focused on sustaining a brisk walking pace when I couldn't. I found that adding in walking breaks actually made me faster than running alone. It wasn't the glorious pace I was hoping to maintain, but it was getting the job done.

As I made it from mile twenty-five to thirty-one, I couldn't help but commend myself for making it to the ultra-distance. I rejoiced at the fact that I completed a 50k in this extreme heat and humidity. The victory dance didn't last too long, because soon after the 50k mark, I became hyper aware of just how bad my feet had become.

Between miles thirty-one to forty, I had to walk a lot more than I could run. The spirit was strong, but the body just wasn't willing. The sun had finally pounded me into submission and my feet felt like balloons that were slowly expanding inside my shoes. Every part of my step was uncomfortable.

The blisters on my toes rubbed the insides of my shoes until they were completely raw. The sensation these blisters caused felt like bee stings on the tips of my toes. The pads of my feet were still very soggy, and I was confused as to whether the squishy sensation on the bottom of my foot was due to them being waterlogged or if the entire bottom of my foot was a blister. Either way the sensation it caused felt like walking on a hot road with the bottom of my foot being sunburned. Between the soaking wet shoe and the scorching heat of the asphalt, I was in essence cooking my feet.

As my pain tolerance decreased so did my self-esteem. The creeping thought of not finishing kept prodding my mind, looking for a soft spot to infiltrate. During this section of the race, the only thing that kept me going forward was positive self-talk, even if I didn't fully believe it, and noticing that other runners in this section appeared to be struggling with the same difficulties.

Even though I didn't want anything but success for the other runners on the course, I did find peace knowing that I wasn't alone in the struggle. I guess the age-old saying "misery loves company" is a true statement.

As I approached the mile forty aid station and check-in point, I looked forward to changing my socks and shoes again. I phoned ahead to Leigh-Ann and asked her to have a dry set of socks and my trail-running shoes available.

The KEYS 100 is one hundred percent on paved roadways and bike trails. There was no need for trail shoes, but I looked forward to the change of impact on my foot that the tread of the trail shoes would offer. Even though Leigh-Ann was still consistently meeting me every one to two miles, it didn't feel like enough.

I felt lost and adrift on the course, in a sea of my own sorrow and self-pity. The only beacon of hope that I had was that a change of socks and shoes would hopefully equate to a change of heart and mind.

Finally arriving at the mile forty aid station, I made my way to the van and promptly plopped down in a chair that Leigh-Ann had set up. As I lifted my battered legs to remove my socks and shoes, my I.T. bands and quadriceps felt like they were going to rip.

I looked at Leigh-Ann with the most pitiful puppy dog eyes I could muster and asked for help with removing my shoes. After freeing my feet from their swampy prison, I decided I needed to assess the carnage. I knew there was nothing positive to gain from looking at my feet, but like passing a train wreck I had to take a peek.

GOOD LORD was that a mistake!

My feet looked as if they had been floating in the ocean for days while hungry sea creatures nibbled on them. Leigh-Ann did her best to try to remain positive and break the tension, while my mom stood in concerned silence, and my amazing nine-year-old daughter walked away and pretended like she was going to throw-up. I looked at Leigh-Ann and in an exacerbated attempt to make light of the situation said, "Well, at least they are still attached. I guess that's a plus."

As I struggled to get my new set of Injinji toe socks on, one of the race officials and racecourse medics walked by and noticed my feet.

He was taken back by the sight of the pale prunes at the ends of my legs. He asked my wife if I had dropped from the race, and he seemed shocked to find out that I was headed back out. He looked at me and said, "Buddy, your feet look like hamburger meat. I have seen plenty of people today who have dropped for far less, so good luck to you."

With that heart-warming encouragement, I was either ready to get back to running or throw myself into traffic. I decided it would be less effort to just jump back on the course and ride the struggle bus as far as I could.

After wrestling my dry socks onto my wet feet, I slid them into my trail shoes. I felt a moment of relief, as they were not applying pressure in the same places as my first pair.

After Leigh-Ann helped me up from the chair, I started limping my way back to the course in an attempt to wake my legs back up. Leigh-Ann asked if there was anything else I needed. I asked her for one of my shot-sized energy drinks. She handed me the small bottle, and I placed it into my pocket and planned to use it as I made my way down the course.

Walking away from my crew, I asked Leigh-Ann what I should expect in the next section. She told me that I had ten miles to the halfway point. She further explained that the next section I needed to overcome before making it there would be a lovely little place called Hell's Tunnel. I didn't even hesitate when I said in an exacerbated and sarcastic response, "Fan-FUCKING-tastic!"

Part 3

Miles Forty to Sixty: Hell's Tunnel and the Seven Mile Bridge

Making my way back on the course, I felt like a soldier returning to battle. I slowly increased my pace until my feet were shuffling in a quick, choppy stride. As my legs started to wake back up from their short vacation of sitting down, I noticed that my feet were not hurting as badly. Don't get me wrong, they still were far from comfortable, but they weren't agonizing. I decided to capitalize on the slight relief by increasing my pace to a running stride.

After slowly running for a couple of miles and meeting back up with my crew to refill my water bottles and pack me down with ice, I came across a small sign on the side of the paved trail that was staked into the ground welcoming us to Hell's Tunnel. Looking down the trail was very intimidating; the sun-scorched overgrowth of the marsh looked like an apocalyptic swamp.

Mustering the courage to press on, my breath was immediately pulled from my chest when I entered the stale, dank brush line. After running about one hundred yards into it, it dawned on me that the heat and humidity was not the only challenge. The smell from the soggy marshland lingered in the air and made me feel like I was running through a compost pile.

The one part that was pretty cool was watching the large

crabs dart across the trail as I was approaching. There was one group of crabs that were feasting on a decomposing carcass. I was unsure if it was a possum or a racoon; my only goal was to make sure I didn't succumb to Hell's Tunnel in the same way.

Roughly a half-mile in, the panic that I had left at the last aid station caught back up with me. I stopped for a second to pull myself together and do my best to take a deep breath. As I came to a standstill, the humid air surrounded me and hugged me like a straight-jacket. I found it hard to even expand my lungs in this area.

Starting to walk again, I remembered my energy drink in my pocket, and I thought to myself, *What the hell, why not?*

I unscrewed the top and downed the entire shot bottle. Then I went right back to placing one foot in front of the other.

After about five minutes had passed, I felt a tingling sensation come over me and I knew that the caffeine had started to kick in. I instantly felt my spirit uplift as my legs rose to the occasion. I went from barely dragging my swollen sausage feet down the trail to running the same pace I would maintain at a local 5k. The energy shot may as well have been jet fuel.

As I burned my way through the remainder of Hell's Tunnel, I passed two other runners who complimented me on how strong I looked. As I humbly passed them, I offered the best words of encouragement that I could muster in the moment.

After clearing the final section of marshy brush line, I saw my crew parked in the grass. All three of my crew members were surprised at just how strong I looked. It was a much-needed confidence boost to see their reactions to my appearance.

As I continued to ride the coattails of my energy drink, I

quickly topped off my water bottles, packed my shirt with ice yet again, and placed my lighted running vest and head lamp on as I prepared for sunset. I briskly took off and continued down the course towards the halfway point — Marathon, Florida.

The following three miles are pretty blurry. I retreated into myself, let my mind wander, and set my body and legs to autopilot. However, I do remember stopping for a minute or two to take pictures of one of the most amazing ocean sunsets I have ever seen before quickly returning to running.

Cruising down the course, I passed through the mile fifty aid station and check-in point still feeling strong. About a half-mile past that aid station, I approached the familiar entrance of our resort, and I could see our room from the course. I began to daydream about making a sharp right-hand turn and running directly into the safety of my hotel bed. Thank God my legs were once again on autopilot as they carried me right past that temptation.

The second it registered in my brain just how far I had actually made it, exhaustion set in. I became ridiculously tired, alarmingly fast. The strong run–walk intervals that I was maintaining morphed into a strong walk–stumble ratio. It was almost nine thirty at night, and I had been running for about thirteen hours. I was now setting a personal record for distance and time on my feet with every step I took.

To say that the two and half miles leading up to the Seven Mile Bridge were sketchy would be a gross understatement. My brain was exhausted as it struggled to make sense of the deep darkness that replaced the bright and sunny skies.

Running down the sidewalk, I noticed a photographer on the course taking my picture. He was really into it, as he was changing positions while staying in place to obtain better action angles. So, I threw a thumbs up and posed for pictures as I ran towards him.

Approaching the photographer, I was shocked to discover that it wasn't a photographer at all: it was actually a mailbox shaped like a manatee. I stopped for a second to connect the dots and literally laughed out loud when I figured out that I had had my first run-induced hallucination. I thought to myself, *well shit, this should make the run across the bridge even more interesting.*

I pulled myself together and gained composure before approaching my crew. Anxieties were high for every runner and their support at this particular section, including mine.

I was about to set foot onto the Seven Mile Bridge, and this would be the section of the race that was un-crewable once you entered. Aside from the other runners staggering down the shoulder of the bridge, I would be completely alone. Leigh-Ann and my mother were both one big ball of nerves. It was terrifying to think that I would be on an ill-lit bridge for seven miles with nothing but a lighted vest to warn speeding drivers of my presence.

The bridge is in the top ten longest bridges in the United States and top three in the list of things I feared about this course. It was only third to not finishing and dying of a heat stroke. Going into this race, I set two goals for myself. First and foremost was to cross the finish line, and the second was to make it over the Seven Mile Bridge before sunset. Seeing that it was about ten thirty at night, at this point, one of these goals was completely lost. My only hope and focus was to not lose the other. With that thought and sentiment, I grabbed my hydration vest, kissed Leigh-Ann and Hannah, put on a brave face and headed into what looked like a black abyss.

The plan while I was on the bridge was for me to stay alive and my crew to go back to the resort, freshen up and prepare for what would turn out to be one of the hardest nights of our lives.

The bridge was as terrifying as I feared in my brain. All my training and preparation leading up to this race was done on the road, and I regularly ran in bicycle lanes and shoulders facing oncoming traffic. I was very acclimated to running confidently while vehicles drove past. However, there is no amount of preparation that can prepare you for the experience of running on the Seven Mile Bridge at night.

As vehicles approached, I would shake my headlamp back and forth, praying that the oncoming vehicles would see me. Thinking back to my days as a paramedic, I wondered how many of these drivers were completely intoxicated. My mind couldn't help but picture what the scene would look like if I were even clipped by one of these speeding vehicles. I found minimal comfort in the dark, sarcastic thought that if I were to get hit I probably wouldn't even feel anything.

As cars sped by, some vehicles chose to turn their high beams on and blind me. Some would roll their windows down and scream at the runners. Some would swerve back and forth as if it was funny to make the runners think that they were going to be hit, but for the majority of the vehicles, you would notice a sudden deceleration as the vehicles scooted as far as they could to the left to give us a wide berth.

The halfway point of the bridge was a very confusing section. You were far enough away from the beginning and the end to feel like you were stuck in a moonlit purgatory.

Once again, my brain started to fill in gaps out of pure exhaustion. I had an extremely weird moment while I was looking at the sky as the moon bounced off the few clouds that were present. My entire view became pixelated, and it was almost like every section of the sky and water was formed by Lego building blocks. I knew the pattern was some type of hallucination as I tried to reattach myself to reality. Being this exhausted in the middle of emptiness, while four-door missiles flew past at what felt like five hundred miles per hour, was cause for concern.

I remembered Dean Karnazes speaking in one of his books about being so tired during a run that he wandered into traffic. I knew that if this happened to me, I would wander into the grill of one of the oncoming vehicles.

In an attempt to refocus my mind and uplift my spirit I placed my headphones on and started to play an old Steve Harvey stand-up comedy special. This was exactly what I needed, and before long I found myself cracking up at the well-delivered punch lines. It not only helped to ease my fear and nerves, but his jokes also took my mind off the pain and turbulence that was building in my body. It was just enough encouragement to carry me through the last half of the Seven Mile Bridge.

As I saw a collective cluster of headlights in the distance, I knew I was approaching the mile sixty aid station. Leigh-Ann had called me a couple of times while I was on the bridge to ensure my safety and to let me know they were anxiously awaiting my arrival.

Approaching the end of the bridge, my comedy special came to an end as well as the adrenaline that was carrying me through the fear of dying. Walking off that bridge, I felt one hundred percent drained. My legs were involuntarily spasming as dizziness and nausea took over my brain. I checked in with the race officials and made my way to my crew.

Now that the Seven Mile Bridge was behind me, I could speak honestly of how it made me feel. I am unsure if it was the fatigue, exhaustion or delusion of being in so much pain, but once I saw Leigh-Ann, I started sobbing. I confessed that this was the hardest thing I had ever done, and that bridge was one of the scariest experiences of my life.

Tears were rolling down Leigh-Ann's face as she welcomed me to mile sixty. She tried to hold it together for my benefit and not let me see how worried she was at my appearance.

I told her that I had overcome the two hardest sections of the course, Hell's Tunnel and the Seven Mile Bridge. I went on to tell her that the hard parts were over and that I would just need to maintain a reasonable pace and cruise to the finish line. Unknown to me, those two sections were "cake" compared to the next obstacle I would have to overcome... myself.

Chapter Twelve

Part 1

On the Line

"You'll be wistful for the 'wall' of the marathon, when you hit the 'death grip' of the ultra."
- Bob Glover

Leaving the mile sixty aid station was a challenge in itself. My emotions were becoming more and more unstable as the fatigue beat me into the ground. I remember looking at Leigh-Ann while sobbing, "I don't want to do this anymore. Please don't make me go back out there."

Being my rock, Leigh-Ann responded, "It's only another two miles before you see us again and then you will have made it to the 100k mark."

I could tell that she was fighting back tears and putting on a brave face to push me along the course. In the months leading up to the race, I prepared everybody in my crew for the possibility of witnessing me implode on myself.

I was collapsing in on myself faster than a dying star. I made each of my crew members, especially Leigh-Ann, promise me that they would not allow me to quit because of fatigue or pain. If you were to ask Leigh-Ann, to this day, she would tell you that this was one of the hardest promises she has ever had to keep.

After receiving my stern direction, I was too tired to protest. I left my hydration vest with them, grabbed my hand-held water bottle and continued on my quest for a triple digit finish.

As I trudged my way down the course, I tried my hardest to focus on silver linings of the race. I kept telling myself that with the moon in the sky the race would be less intense. I knew that the sun wouldn't be back to wreak havoc on me for hours. To my surprise, the sun would have been a welcome challenge compared to the nuisance of the mosquitoes and biting gnats that plagued me.

The biting insects feasted on me in droves during this section of the race. By the time I made it to mile sixty-two to meet my crew, it felt as if I had lost a liter of blood to the tiny vampires that descended upon me. I called ahead to Leigh-Ann to let her know that I would need bug spray, and before I could even get that out, she asked, "What the hell is up with all these bugs!"

Apparently, I was not the only one they were targeting. As I made it to my crewing van, I found Leigh-Ann and my mother flailing their arms as they tried to fight off the pestilence. The other runners at this crewing point were also enduring the same battle we were.

I can honestly say I have never been surrounded by so many insects in my life. We all had bugs flying in our ears, up our noses, up our shorts, getting stuck in our eyelashes and gnawing on every square inch of exposed skin.

When the van door would open, they would flood in towards the light, filling the vehicle with hundreds of tiny flying teeth. The luckiest one on the course that night was Hannah, because she was asleep in the van and completely covered with a blanket from head to toe. She may have well been wearing the cloak of invisibility. For us however, it was hell!

I cannot stress enough the frustration and irritation this number of insects brought. The best way to describe the number of mosquitos and biting gnats was biblical. I doubt if Pharaoh even dealt with a plague of this magnitude.

While at this crewing spot, my wife handed me a can of bug spray, and I promptly started to spray myself from my head to my toes. Unfortunately, the relief was short-lived. I felt like the insects looked at the bug spray like steak sauce enriching the flavor of a prime cut piece of meat.

While my mom was busy spraying the area around the three of us, Leigh-Ann was trying to force me to eat. It had been a few hours since I had eaten anything of note. I was struggling with extreme nausea since completing the Seven Mile Bridge.

It was so bad that holding down water became a challenge. Leigh-Ann tried a couple of different items, including trail mix, some gummy worms and a couple other treats to stimulate my appetite. Nothing seemed to be working, until my eyes caught sight of a cheeseburger from McDonald's that was purchased a few hours earlier. It was the only thing in our vehicle that sounded halfway appetizing.

I asked Leigh-Ann if I could have the cheeseburger. She quickly grabbed it and handed it to me. At this point, my mom had cultivated an entire atmosphere of aerosol bug spray. It was creating a slight forcefield against the aerial attacks.

As I took a couple of bites of the cheeseburger, the mechanics of chewing was too much for my mind to handle. The texture and taste of the chewed food resting on my tongue instantly stirred a revolt in my stomach.

Before I could even warn anyone of the rebellion taking place in my gut, every last chucky ounce of stomach content came flying out of my face. I had a projectile stream of vomit rushing out of my mouth and both nostrils. It was a surreal and almost cartoonish force and amount. The fountain of bile made it about five feet from where I was standing. As it splashed on the side of the road, it only took seconds for it to attract a swarm of insects that was captured by the glow of our taillights.

I watched as my mom and Leigh-Ann stared at me in shock. Neither one of them knew what to say to bring any comfort to this situation, as if there would have been anything that could have been said to make sense of this nightmare.

Before I could even muster words, the aftershock of the violent force hit me like a baseball bat. My back and abdomen spasmed viciously as I cried out in agony. I locked eyes with Leigh-Ann and saw the amount of concern and fear as she saw the amount of hopelessness and despair.

I was at mile sixty-two and felt completely unhinged.

I told Leigh-Ann that this was useless, and I just needed to keep going. I didn't allow my brain to even process the terrible shape I was in. All I knew was that I felt like failure was imminent.

I decided right then that if I was destined to fail, it wouldn't be in this spot, so I continued forward on the course. With the lingering feeling of defeat looming over my head, I made the executive decision to fail forward. If my body was completely falling apart, it might as well fall apart as I was making my way closer to the finish line.

Leaving that crewing station was one of the most confusing moments of my life. My brain felt disconnected from my body as it tried to figure out what was going on. The different parts of my mind felt as if they had broken out into study groups and were all working independently and not as one.

One group was trying to figure out what the hell was going on. Another was trying to figure out what exactly was after us and the last group was just trying to keep me moving forward without dropping to the fetal position and going to sleep.

Moving down the course feeling completely dissociated with reality made me feel like a zombie from *The Walking Dead*. My pace was agonizingly slow as I sauntered into the darkness of US-1.

Within about a quarter mile, my new friends were back. I was once again covered in blood-sucking insects. To be honest, it was a blessing in disguise. Every time my autonomic response slapped my face in an attempt to kill bugs, it jolted me awake and produced a micro-dose of adrenaline.

These little bumps of energy were the only thing carrying me the following mile, where I would once again meet up with my crew. This time I would be sure to carry bug spray on me as I left.

After what felt like an eternity of sluggish stop and go with my crew, Leigh-Ann told me that the next stop would be the mile seventy aid station. I couldn't believe it: I had less than a 50k before finishing this trial by hellfire. That last mile before making my way into the aid station, I felt a jolt of invigoration. There is an old saying within the ultra-community that says, "If you ever feel good in a one hundred-miler, give it time and it will pass. Likewise, if you ever feel bad in a one hundred-miler, give it time and it will pass."

I felt newfound energy coursing through my muscles as I slowly picked up the speed and maintained a strong, yet cautious, pace and running cadence as I approached the aid station and check point.

After announcing my bib number to the course marshal, I walked over to the crewing van and sat down for about eight minutes while I toweled off the sweat and bug spray that had been streaming in my eyes for the last couple of hours.

The nausea that I felt earlier had run its course and I felt capable of holding down some much-needed calories. I nibbled on some cashews as Leigh-Ann made me a hearty PB and J sandwich. My taste buds were convinced that I was dining on a five-star meal as I ate that plain PB and J on the side of that black road. Anyone who has ever run super-long distances knows that you can hit a stage of hunger that can make the most mundane foods seem gourmet.

After eating the king's meal and discussing the next section of the race, I realized that I had been sitting longer than I would have liked. A crew stop that should have taken two to five minutes ended up lasting about fifteen.

Scared that my ass was actually taking root, I tried to lift myself back to my feet as I prepared for my glorious return to battle.

Watching me stand up was like watching a baby deer take its first steps. My hips locked up like the Tin Man, pre-oil can. My knees wobbled and shook like I was paddleboarding on the Bering Strait. My ankles radiated a sharp pain up my legs that seemed to trick my brain into thinking I had stepped in one of those old school bear traps. Finally, my feet — my poor, poor feet. They were swollen to about twice their normal size and felt as if they were on the verge of splitting right down the middle.

Within a fraction of a second after successfully standing, I knew I was in terrible shape.

I tried not to let my wife and my mom see the true pain I was experiencing so, I quickly and instinctively put on a brave face. I told them that I would see them in about two miles and that I was feeling good as I walked away. Once I was far enough from them to ensure they couldn't see nor hear me, I lost it! I completely and utterly broke down into an all-out sob fest.

Every emotion that a human can feel, I had experienced multiple times up to this point. As I walked and stumbled forward, my emotions became completely untethered.

The physical pain that I was feeling, mixed with the emotional exhaustion I was experiencing, created one of the deepest and darkest despairs of my life. Even though I knew there were other runners on the course, marshals patrolling and a loving crew never more than one to two miles away, I felt completely alone. As I continued to push through the darkness of the course, I also explored the dark areas in my mind that I had tried so hard to ignore over the years.

This portion of the race was like intense flames bringing all my impurities to the surface. I sobbed uncontrollably as I reflected on my life and all the mistakes that I had made over the years. I thought about all the stress and pain that I put Leigh-Ann through and her feelings of hopelessness as I attempted to slowly kill myself with alcohol and drugs. My heart and mind joined forces and cried out as one as I thought about the asshole that I was before getting sober.

My body continued to propel me forward as my heart and mind was paralyzed in a state of anguish. Moving forward, every step I took felt violent. My only reprieve was the six or seven times I briefly met my crew during the stretch between miles seventy and eighty.

Around mile seventy-seven, a glimmer of hope peeked over the horizon as the first signs of a new sunrise came into view. I guess the saying is correct when people state, "It is always darkest right before dawn."

Memories and traumas from my past that were tucked away in dormant emotions were now exposed by the light. I knew I was at a pivotal point, not just in the race, but in my life. I knew that the only way that I was going to be able to move forward was by digging deep and finding some measure of positivity to cling to.

I was completely unsure of where this positivity was going to come from as I death-marched on the side of US-1. My body was all but literally falling apart. Every nerve ending below my waist was sounding the alarm to stop before permanent damage was done. My brain reminded me that it had taken about four and a half hours to travel only ten miles.

At this point, I was walking on the outside edges of my feet, taking about forty-five minutes per mile. I was just trying to make it to the mile eighty aid station as if my life depended on it.

After meeting with Leigh-Ann one last time, she told me I only had about a half mile to go.

As she drove the short distance ahead to meet up at the aid station, I called her on the phone. I instantly broke down and told her that I didn't think I could continue after mile eighty.
I told her that my feet felt as if I were walking on live electrical wires. She asked me what she could do to help, and I told her to please call one of the course medics to come and take a look at my feet. Before quickly hanging up with me, she said that she would have them waiting. After realizing that it was going to take me another twenty to thirty minutes at this pace to reach

my destination and see a medic, all I could quietly repeat to myself was, *holy shit! God, please help me...what the hell am I doing? I am so damn stupid...I am so damn stupid...I am so damn stupid! God, if you just get me through this, then never again!*

Part 2

Mile Eighty Triumph: Boundless

I'm not saying that I have ever summited Mount Everest. All I'm saying is that I understand the gratification of those who have. As my broken body peaked over the bridge lying directly in front of the mile eighty aid station, my brain felt every inch of its ten-foot elevation gain.

I could see my wife anxiously waiting before she made her way to meet me. When she approached, I could see tears in her eyes, and I knew I must have looked horrible for her to start crying at the mere sight of me. I slid my handheld water bottle off, exposing all the blisters that lay under its strap.

Leigh-Ann informed me that she had been speaking to the two race marshals at the aid station, Tony and Denise. She went on to advise me that the medic had just arrived moments earlier and was ready to look at my feet. I continued to hobble the last few yards until I was able to collapse into a camping chair in front of the medic and his box of supplies.

After exchanging pleasantries, he asked me, "So, how are you doing?"

I tried to think of something witty and clever to say but my frazzled brain capitalized on the opportunity to send out an S.O.S. I looked him square in the eyes, and in a moment of full honesty and sincerity replied, "I think that I'm dying."

He chuckled and waited for me to crack a smile, but in that

moment, I truly believed the flat statement.

As he reached down to assist my legs to the propped-up position on a second camping chair, I swear I felt every muscle fiber in my legs stretch like a sun-rotted rubber band on the verge of ripping in half.

I think that I was actually surprised when my muscles didn't detach from my bones. My hamstrings felt like steel cables as they pulled on my lower back. The only word that even comes close to describing the feeling of that position was agony.

I watched carefully as the medic untied my shoes and carefully slipped them off my sausage feet. He slowly and delicately peeled the blood-soaked sock off each foot. It felt as if he were peeling the top layers of skin instead of the sock. If I didn't see each sock come off with my own two eyes, I would have sworn that the fibers of the sock were actually fused to my foot.

Each foot was a complete and perfect mess. As Leigh-Ann stood behind him, I watched the horror reflect from her face. My mother, who was standing next to her, gasped in shock.

The medic raised his eyebrows while he studied my feet. Then he looked up at me and bluntly said, "These things are FUBAR."

Having seen many "FUBAR" things in my career as a first responder, I was intimately familiar with its meaning.

My feet were in fact... *Fucked Up Beyond All Recognition.*

I adjusted my hips in the chair so that I could lean forward and witness the disaster myself. Both feet were glowing red and had blisters everywhere.

On the outsides of my feet, I had large fluid-filled sacs that resembled extra deformed toes. I noticed a large white flap of loose skin hanging between the big toe and second toe on my right foot. My left foot was just as bad, if not worse. My heel resembled a piece of abstract organic art with its bumpy, blistered texture.

There was a large sliver of skin missing from the base of my toe and extending to the arch of my foot. I couldn't help but dwell on the idea that I had a Band-Aid-sized flap of skin floating around my sock somewhere.

Both feet were about one shoe size larger due to all the swelling. Wiggling my toes made the bottom of my feet feel like they were going to split down the middle. It seems like a cynical thought, but I knew in my heart that the only way this medic could have helped me would have been by performing a Civil War-style amputation right there on the side of the road.

After carefully forming a plan of attack, he took a large safety pin and began to treat my foot as a pin cushion. He poked the large blisters and they erupted as if they were carbonated. They quickly flattened out as they started to become recognizable again.

As he moved to the bottom, the pain became unbearable. The pads of my feet were the perfect shelter for large blisters underneath. I had multiple silver dollar-sized blisters that were perfectly protected by this area.

The medic, bless his heart, tried every approach that he could to penetrate these thickened parts of my feet. Every millimeter he advanced the safety pin felt as if he were driving a hot roofing nail completely through my foot

As I winced and groaned in pain, you could see his anxiety rise. After exhausting every measure, he finally threw in the white flag. He looked at me with complete defeat in his eyes and said, "The pads of your feet are just way too thick, and I

251

can't reach the blisters underneath. All I can do is tape your feet and we can hope that they don't get any worse."

I looked past him as I accepted his bleak prognosis. Tony, one of the race marshals who had been steadily watching me during my roadside surgery, walked over and said encouragingly, "You know, this is a really tough race, and making it this far is very respectable, especially in this heat."

I knew that he was respectfully hinting that I was pretty much out of the race at this point. Leigh-Ann joined in and told the marshal, "He has done amazingly, with this being his first one hundred-miler attempt."

The marshal looked back at me and said, "That's incredible that this is your first one hundred and you chose to attempt the Keys."

He went on to say that if I was going to drop, now would be the time. My crew was here, the sun was starting to really heat back up, and based on the state of my feet, nobody would question my decision.

I sat there with a blank stare as I digested all the variables that went along with this decision. I thought about everything that was on the line. It wasn't just the twenty-six hours I had spent running this course or the amount of people I told about the attempt; it wasn't just the ten months of hardcore training and focus or the financial and time investments...

Ultimately, my self-respect was on the line.

During this race, I had overcome the heat, distance and a whole slew of obstacles. I faced the sun, speeding cars, trippy visualizations and enough mosquitoes to carry off a small water buffalo. These were all just minor inconveniences to the obstacle that was currently rearing its ugly face.

This race brought all my inner demons and trauma to the

surface. I was not only staring face-to-face at all of my shortcomings; I was once again looking face-to-face at my internal mirror.

Over the years of my life, I knew what it was to like and respect the person looking back, but I also knew what it was like to despise him.

There was so much more than a race and a belt buckle on the line. I was on the line.

I thought back to the vow that I had made to my crew and myself before starting the race.

I would either finish this race, run out of time or get picked up by an ambulance. Quitting is not an option!

Since I wasn't at the finish line, there was still time on the clock, and the rescue wagon wasn't on its way. The choice was clear: there was only one direction to go and that was forward.

I told the marshal that I was not going to drop and that I wanted to get back onto the course. He glanced down at his watch and looked up in a combination of respect and scepticism and told me bluntly, "If you are going to continue on, you have to leave NOW."

He told me that the person in the official last place had left the aid station about ten minutes ago. It had been roughly forty-five minutes since I had planted myself in this chair and I was almost certain that my ass had taken root.

The medic slid my blood- and serum-soaked socks back onto my feet before I wedged them back into my battle-worn shoes. Then he extended his hand to help me out of my cozy camping chair.

As I replanted my feet on the asphalt and lifted myself to a standing position, my body creaked, popped and screamed in instant affliction. I sucked up the shock and placed a brave face on. Both Tony and Denise told me again that I needed to get a move on now.

Leigh-Ann looked at me in complete admiration and told me how proud she was of me. She told me she would drive one mile ahead and pull over to wait for me, to make sure I didn't need anything. I kissed her on the forehead before starting back on my journey. As I walked away from that aid station, I knew I was a different person. I was proud to be back on my feet no matter how bad they hurt.

After making it about twenty yards back down the course, my brain resumed its attack.

"YOU HAVE ANOTHER TWENTY MILES, YOU IDIOT... YOU CAN'T POSSIBLY THINK YOU CAN MAKE IT ON THESE FEET!"

My feet were on fire. It felt like the medic had soaked my socks in gasoline and filled them with Lego bricks and broken glass before replacing them. I studied the pain signals that my brain was receiving and realized that I was still standing. I accepted that the pain felt terrible, but it wasn't killing me... *the pain only hurt*!

I refocused on the road... not the road in front of me, but the road behind me. I started reflecting on my life and all the events that had brought me to this point. I remembered the depressing lows and suicidal thoughts that I had struggled with for so many years.

I remembered all the hell and self-hatred I had endured while I looked in the mirror and truly hated the person who was looking back.

I remembered isolating myself into bathrooms to shoot up opiates, because they helped me cope with the overwhelming anger and depression I was experiencing.

I remembered drinking liquor until my body would literally reject it and my liver would scream in pain, all because I just wanted to be numb.

I remembered the look in my wife's eyes while she gazed upon me with tears forming and told me that she was no longer sure if she could stand by my side if I continued my kamikaze course.

I remembered all the agony I went through and what REAL suffering was.

Instantly, while standing in the relentless sun as vehicles whizzed by, surrounded by some of the most beautiful scenery this earth has to offer, I decided that I would no longer run out of desperation and fear but instead gratitude. After all, I had every reason in the world to be thankful...

Here I was, sober, happy, current physical pain aside of course, standing in a literal paradise and surrounded by the people that I loved the most in this world, people who were loving enough to sit in a minivan for over twenty-four hours to crew me up to this point.

Yeah, I might be in pain physically, but it was a welcome change to the many years I had spent as a numb, lifeless shell of myself.

I started to focus on all the things I was thankful for, and as I shifted my outlook of my current situation, my pace shifted as well. I went from a death march to a walk. From a walk to a shuffle. A shuffle to a trot and finally a trot to a full-on run.

As my pace picked up, so did my pain tolerance and optimism. Before long I felt as if I were flying.

I ended up making it to the mile marker where Leigh-Ann was planning to meet me before she could even make it there.

She pulled up right as I was passing the point. She called me on the phone, surprised, and asked if I needed anything. I told her I was good and that I just wanted to get this race done.

For the next nine miles, I maintained a ridiculously strong pace, considering my overall condition. I had my desire and drive zeroed in. My crew had my support down to an art. Leigh-Ann would drive ahead a couple of miles and pull over. My mom would help prep supplies so that Leigh-Ann could run them down the course to me as I was approaching. This completely negated the need to stop at all.

One of my strongest driving factors was now completely awake and in all-out cheerleader mode. I could hear Hannah screaming and cheering for me as I came into sight of each crewing spot. The fact that my daughter was proud of me was enough to keep me moving forward through any physical condition. I knew I wasn't only proving a point to myself; I was also proving to my daughter that you can complete anything that you set your mind to.

Approaching the mile ninety marker, I had built up a little bit of a time buffer. It was about eleven o'clock in the morning when I entered that aid station. Tony and Denise were both there waiting as well.

Both of them commented on how strong I looked and how impressed they were with my comeback. Unfortunately for me, the mathematical part of my brain was not fully functional. When the race official at mile ninety told me that I only had three and a half hours to finish this race, my brain went into an all-out frenzy.

I topped off my water bottles and took off running even harder than I had for the previous ten miles. The thought that I could make it to mile ninety and then run out of time before finishing was terrifying!

Running down that sidewalk with a ten-to-twelve-minute mile was nothing short of a miracle, especially for the shape that I was in. My feet stung and burned as I felt the drained blister sacks shearing and tearing off in my shoes.

The now separated flaps of skin and raw lining of my foot created a slippery surface inside my shoe. As I felt my feet slide around in their own blood and sweat, I dug in deep and continued to press on. I couldn't help but think to myself, what would David Goggins say to me at this moment? He would probably tell me to shut the fuck up and work harder. And that is EXACTLY what I did.

Other than the guttural war cries and grunts that escaped my mouth every third to fourth step, I ran with laser-locked focus. I continued to increase my pace over the next five miles. I started to catch and pass other runners in the race. This section of the race is a little blurry, but I am pretty sure I caught and passed approximately ten to fifteen runners.

Approaching mile ninety-five, Leigh-Ann was standing at the entrance of a gas station with Tony and Denise. Leigh-Ann was crying as I approached. She was completely stunned by how strong I looked.

As she handed me a freshwater bottle, she kept telling me that I was going to finish. The moment she told me that I had two and a half hours to make it the remaining five miles, I instantly broke down.

Even with my mind being completely unhinged, I could do this math. I started to sob in relief, but before I could get too emotional, Tony interrupted me and said, "It's not time for this yet; you need to get moving."

I received his words like a little peewee football player

would take orders from a coach. I took the fresh water bottle and a pineapple popsicle and once again took off running.

Running the next few miles almost seemed effortless and borderline enjoyable. I maintained a strong pace and used this time to express my gratitude in the form of reflection and prayer.

After making it to mile ninety-seven to ninety-eight, I was done. Not with the race physically but mentally.

The last stretch took place in crowded Key West, directly on the waterfront. It was a busy section of the beach as I made my way down the sidewalk resembling a battle-worn warrior returning to civilization.

My mind was completely unraveled and incapable of processing any information other than relentless forward progress. I continued to put one foot in front of the other as my mind taunted me and told me that the finish line was moving further and further away.

In a sudden acute state of paranoia, I called Leigh-Ann at around mile ninety-nine and told her that I was scared that I was lost. She told me that was impossible, because there was only one direction I could be heading and that was toward the finish.

Her voice alone calmed my mind and brought me peace. She asked if I wanted the crew to start walking towards my position and meet me before the finish line. I cried out in the mousiest pathetic voice, "Yes, please."

Right after hanging up, I picked up my pace and started running so I could see them sooner. Making my way down the final street before the finishers chute, I saw my crew.

Even though I had literally been surrounded by paradise for the majority of the run, this moment was one of the most beautiful sights. Hannah ran to me and hugged me before telling me, "The finish line is right there, Daddy."

I had less than a quarter mile to go and about forty-five minutes to make it. As we walked that little distance, runners that I had just passed started to overtake me. Leigh-Ann asked if I wanted to run the final few feet and cross the finish line on my own. I quickly protested by saying, "Hell no, we are all crossing this finish line together. After all, I don't think first place is on the line."

We all laughed as we turned the final corner onto Higgs Beach and looked dead at the finish line arch, about twenty yards away. Air horns started to sound as spectators began to cheer. I took Leigh-Ann and Hannah's hands in each one of mine as we approached and crossed the finish line with tears rolling. As I stood on the line, Bob Becker presented me with a teal belt buckle and medal with a parrot on it that read "2019 KEYS 100 Finisher".

I stood there posing for pictures in a complete daze. I knew in my core that I was not the same man who had started this race. I knew that I had gone through an emotional purging on a profound and spiritual level.

I had more than I could have ever imagined on the line during this race as I came out victorious. The belt buckle, medal and bragging rights were an amazing token of success, but I knew my true award was waiting for me in the mirror.

Part 3

Never Say Never

After learning that my official time was 31h:21m:19s, all I wanted was a bed. My crew was fast at work getting the van squared away for the fifty-mile drive back to the resort in Marathon, where we would be staying for one more night. First, I did my best to make my way to a men's restroom that was on the beach that had showers located in it.

As I sat on the restroom bench, I started to peel my grimy and sweat-soaked clothing off my broken body. I felt like a lobster shedding its armored shell and exposing the soft and vulnerable creature inside.

It was the first time in about thirty-three hours that I didn't have compression clothing squeezing me. I made my way to my socks, but I struggled to reach my feet. As I pulled my legs up to me, my hamstrings and quads quivered and screamed in pain. Sitting on that bench, in that public bathroom, I learned that my range of motion was worse than that of an oak tree.

After a few minutes of creative and painful bending, I finally freed my feet from their bloody prison. I left the tape on that the medic had placed, mainly because I couldn't fathom the pain I would endure as I ripped off the tape and adhesive promoter that he used.

I slid on a pair of flip flops that Leigh-Ann had given me and made my way to the shower. Now, any long-distance runner

260

will tell you that hot water and soap will find chafed areas of the body just like hand sanitizer finds paper cuts.

GOOD LORD! Every square inch of my body was chafed except my teeth and fingernails.

That shower may have been the fastest shower that I had ever taken. Due to the sunburn and chafing I was forced to pat dry with my towel. I really can't explain enough that I hurt EVERYWHERE!

Once I was toweled off enough to put dry, loose-fitting clothes on, the real challenge presented itself. It was time for me to get dressed. I'm sure I looked like a drunken homeless contortionist, and to anyone in the men's room that day I deeply apologize.

Upon exiting the locker room, Leigh-Ann had pulled the van around to the curb to minimize my walk. As my limp body plopped into the passenger seat, Leigh-Ann still had tears flowing on her face with happiness for me. Hannah was talking and congratulating me in the pitch that only a nine-year-old girl can hit, and my mom asked me, "So, how do you feel?"

I responded in an exhausted claim of pride, "Alive!"

She went on to ask me jokingly, "When is the next one?"

I almost choked on my words as I quickly replied, "I will NEVER run a hundred miles again! This is for sure a one and done."

Once our exchange was over, we started the sketchy fifty-mile drive back to Marathon. I cannot advise anyone enough to make sure that your crew is properly rested before leaving a finish line.

Thank God Leigh-Ann found the strength to keep our trip back to Marathon from ending in a fiery crash. I can honestly say I have zero recollection of this drive. I do however remember waking up in the parking lot of our resort and knowing that I had to somehow make it the fifty yards from the parking lot to our condo, not to mention the four steps that I would have to free climb in order to get inside.

As I was trying to get out of the van, my entire body was stiff and had taken on the form of the passenger seat. I felt like Abe at the Lincoln Memorial, trying to stand up and exit his chair.

After a lot of mustering of strength and lifting support from Leigh-Ann, I was back on my feet. I carefully and precisely focused on each step along the sidewalk. Once I made it to the stairs of our beach condo, I knew there was no way I was going to be able to climb them with my legs. I used the railing and Leigh-Ann to help lower me to all fours as I began to crawl up the steps, much like an elderly dog that just had a hip replacement.

Leigh-Ann opened the front door and I swear I heard a church choir singing. For a brief moment, I thought the pearly gates to heaven were opening. Making my way through the door, my sights were set on the couch in the living room.

After expending the very last energy stores that my body had, I found myself lying on this little slice of heaven, with my feet propped up. Leigh-Ann pulled off one of the soft bed comforters and tucked me in before making sure I didn't need anything else. I can't confirm this, but I am pretty sure I was asleep before she finished tucking me in.

While I was fast asleep, my family somehow regained their second wind and spent some much-needed relaxation time at the resort pool.

After waking up to a quiet condo a few hours later, my only

thought was that I wanted to see my family. Before leaving for the pool, Leigh-Ann had placed my cell phone on the coffee table next to me, so all I would have to do was reach it and call them. This plan was great in theory, but as I reached for my phone, I realized how sore my arms and back were. Watching me struggle to get to my phone, one may have thought that I had completed the race while walking on my hands.

After using my Jedi-like focus and determination, the phone somehow made it into my hand. I called Leigh-Ann and heard her phone ringing right outside the patio door. Once she realized that I was awake, the three of them made their way back in. After asking how I had slept, they asked if I was hungry.

I WAS STARVING!

We all settled on ordering some calzones from a local pizzeria. After the delivery guy dropped them off, I decided that this was the best meal I had ever eaten.

A couple hours passed as we discussed and replayed that race mile by mile. During our conversation I felt myself death-gripping my finisher's belt buckle. At that point, I completely understood Gollum's obsession with the ring… this buckle was "my precious".

With the conversation wrapping up, it was finally time to head to bed. I was able to lower myself to the floor and crawl into the downstairs bedroom, where a soft queen-sized bed was calling my name. As I made my way into the bedroom, the four of us couldn't help but laugh at my current condition. I was beautifully and wonderfully broken. Reviving my mom's earlier joke, she asked once again when the next one hundred-miler would be. Lifting myself into the bed I told her that, "I have never been more sure of anything in my life when I say I WILL NEVER RUN ONE OF THESE THINGS AGAIN!"

Leigh-Ann tucked me in and kissed me on my forehead as she told me how proud she was of me. I went to sleep knowing that not only was I a different person in my eyes but also in hers.

After a solid night of sleep and a lot of funky dreams about running on the course, I woke up to daylight breaking through our blinds. My entire body seemed stiffer than before. I tried to lay as still as I could until I could figure out a plan to get out of the bed.

As I lay there strategizing, I could feel my bladder screaming for attention. I knew that I only had a few minutes before this pillow-top bed became a waterbed.

After calling for Leigh-Ann's assistance, I realized that they were outside already loading the vehicle in preparation to return home. Making it to the bathroom was all on me.

After lowering myself to the floor again, I crawled to the restroom, barely making it in time. Once I was completely relieved, I changed my focus and determination on standing. I used the sink to help hoist myself up and leaned on it to support my weight. As I looked up, my eyes stared deep into the mirror The poor man in the reflection looked completely beat up and in pain. Even in this obvious state of distress, I was completely elated with my reflection.

I was staring into the eyes of a person that I respected. He had not only proved that he could complete the one hundred-mile distance but had also faced the darkest corners of his soul with gratitude and forgiveness.

After I had washed my face and brushed my teeth, Leigh-Ann came in and helped me get dressed. This was it – our trip to the Florida Keys was now over in a victorious limp to the van.

On our way home, we continued to talk and reminisce about the battle won. I gushed with appreciation and love for my crew. Hannah handed me a small, folded piece of paper and said, "Daddy, I wrote you a note."

Before I was able to read it, Leigh-Ann told me that Hannah had started writing the letter around mile twenty. As I went on to read the letter, my emotions had a complete meltdown. Her little letter read,

"Dear Daddy, congratulations, you just finished the KEYS 100. You kept going when your feet hurt, even though it was hot, and you had blisters it was worth it for the medal. You are inspiring. You are my hero! You are my inspiration! I love you."

My heart exploded with thankfulness! My little girl had never questioned if I was going to finish; she always had faith in her father even when I questioned myself. To this day, that letter is framed and is considered one of my most priceless possessions.

As we talked further about the race and our adventure, I couldn't help but miss it. I know it sounds crazy, but something happened to me out on that course. Something that I can't even explain. I changed during those miles and experienced a version of life that I never knew existed. I was saddened at the thought of only living that experience once.

As I thumbed through my phone, something caught my eye. I asked Leigh-Ann how Daytona Beach in December sounded. She glanced over at me in a complete state of confusion and asked, "What do you mean?"

I told her, "There is this event that sounds kind of interesting."

She glanced back over in silent scepticism, looking for an elaboration. I hesitatingly said, "The Daytona 100 sounds like it could be fun."

Chapter Thirteen

Part 1

Miles to Come...

"We don't heal in isolation, but in community."
- S. Kelley Harrell

The weeks following our arrival home slowly returned us to a sense of normalcy. Although our daily routines returned to our normal day-to-day, I found myself maintaining my heightened level of self-respect. Like a new mother who forgets about the pain of labor, I was left nurturing the joy and elation that the finish line had brought me. The only remnants of the struggle were the soft spots on my feet that were still healing.

I found myself deep within a state of reminiscing and contemplation.

Is this it?

Have I peaked?

Will I ever be able to relive this feeling again?

What's next?

My mind was restless.

It had been weeks since joking with Leigh-Ann about running the Daytona 100 on our drive back from the Keys, but the more and more I thought about it the more I realized this was no longer a joke… it was a yearning.

I started investing my time into researching everything I could find about the run and the logistics involved in running from Jacksonville to Daytona Beach. It didn't take long for me to decide that I wanted to attempt this run in the upcoming December, roughly six months away.

After presenting the idea to Leigh-Ann and explaining that I wasn't sure if I could finish another one-hundred-mile distance, I went on to tell her that I felt a strong pull in my heart to at least try. As per usual, I was met with excitement and support. Within an hour, I was fully signed up for the 2019 Daytona 100.

Shortly after returning to my normal running routine, I dwelled on the fact that I had about six months before the Daytona 100. While in the grand scheme of things six months really isn't that long, having the knowledge that I could complete a one hundred-miler caused me to be restless.

I decided for my upcoming birthday in August that I would run another ultra. Seeing that I was turning thirty-two, I decided to run thirty-two miles in celebration. After about two weeks of making this decision, my old friend, the brain, started to run his mouth. It had been a while since I had heard his smack talk, but staying true to form, he is never completely muzzled. His approach was a little surprising and suspicious. He taunted me by saying, "Thirty-two miles, huh? That's cute. If you are planning on running all day, why not just make it a hundred? Scared you can't do it?"

That little jerk was right; if I did plan on spending the majority of my day running, why not make it a one hundred-miler?

I rashly made the choice to extend my thirty-two-mile run

by a few extra miles. I told Leigh-Ann my plan and discussed the logistics with her.

In my neighborhood, we have a residential loop that is 1.05 miles long. If I ran those ninety-five times, I would complete one hundred miles. We decided that we could use our front yard as race headquarters and an aid station, which I would have access to with every lap if needed. After solidifying the logistics and route that I would be running, I started to wrap my mind around running another one hundred-miler.

As the days passed, I could not stop thinking about the possibility of reinvigorating and reliving the emotions I had received when crossing the finish line in the Keys. Running meant so much to me; it was a literal lifeline returning and restoring a sense of personal purpose to my life. It gave me the confidence that no matter what life threw at me, I could handle it, if I just took it one step at a time. It not only gave me courage to look at the man in the mirror, it also made me look forward to seeing him.

Ultrarunning was not just a hobby to me; it was a healing force. It brought a wholeness and sense of belonging. It introduced me to others who struggled just as hard, in their own ways. It was not just a weekend adventure; it was my community... my tribe. It is who I am... I am an ultra-runner!

While I knew how impactful running had been for me, I couldn't help but wonder if I could use it to help others. I knew that people used their running to earn donations for charitable organizations, but I had no idea where to even begin.

I told my wife that I wanted to use this run to bring awareness to mental health and substance issues among first responders. Being the amazingly supportive person she is, she jumped on the phone with multiple newspapers and media outlets in our area. She told them that I was planning to run one hundred miles in our neighborhood and of my plan to use it to bring awareness to such a needed cause.

They loved the idea!

The two newspapers and local news station said they would be there to cover it. They scheduled a time to sit down to interview me to learn more about the cause. I discussed in depth, my desire to help first responders that struggle with mental health issues and how mental health had been a taboo topic in the field for so many years. I spoke openly about my struggles and journey to get help. I discussed the event, its location and projection for finishing times, but most of all I expressed that it was okay to ask for help.

Also, I mentioned my run to a couple of my work colleagues, who instantly jumped on the support bandwagon. Word spread around my office like wildfire, and before long the marketing team was reaching out to me in order to use this run to bring awareness to the cause. They assigned one of their writers to interview me for a blog that would have the potential to be read by thousands, if not tens of thousands, of firefighters and EMS workers across North America.

It was at that moment I realized that I had taken a bold step with telling so many people about my upcoming event. I have no idea where the bolstered confidence came from, seeing that my last one-hundred-mile attempt almost caused me to implode on myself. I was literally putting myself in a position to have a potential failure that would be widely witnessed. This was a thought the old me would have dwelled on, but my newfound self-esteem reminded me that, as with life, all I needed was to continue putting one foot in front of the other.

I could not believe how quickly everything came together during the three weeks leading up to race day. What started off as a fun solo birthday run turned into an event with media coverage, a charity website and full-on community support. Once my neighborhood and city's fire department heard about the event, the encouragement was astonishing. One of the lieutenants and peer support coordinators arranged to have support from the fire department by having crews show up at different times throughout the duration of the race to run some miles and/or drop off supplies.

The residents of my neighborhood displayed red balloons on every mailbox on my route, and some even placed makeshift aid stations at the end of their driveways. I was sincerely humbled by the fact that one neighborhood run had brought out the best in people and showed what the true sense of community meant.

As race day approached, all the preparations were complete and all that was left was the simple step of running one hundred miles...

Since the original plan was to run on my birthday, I decided that I wanted to run every minute of it. My plan was to start my run at midnight on my birthday and continue to run throughout the entire day. The morning my run was scheduled to start was already hot and humid. My front yard resembled a FEMA disaster relief base, with all my supplies located underneath a pop-up tent on my front lawn. As I waited for the clock to strike midnight, my wife and mom were standing on the start line with me. We talked, in nervous chatter, about all of the challenges that we were going to face and how we would adapt to them. As the clock struck midnight, my feet struck the ground.

I made my first lap around my quiet and tranquil

neighborhood, and I was shocked to see how many of my neighbors were actually standing in their driveways to briefly cheer for me before heading inside to squeeze in some sleep before waking up for work. After about three miles, the first fire engine crew arrived to meet with me and show their support.

This would be the first crew out of many that would arrive and help make this event profoundly touching. After meeting with them for a few minutes and talking with them a little about my cause, it was time for me to return to the sleepy streets of my course.

During the next eighteen miles, I slipped into a comfortable pace as I navigated my quiet streets with only the occasional passer-by honking in support. Around mile twenty, my first impromptu pacer showed up to knock out some miles. From this point, it was a rare occasion to find me running alone for the remaining miles ahead.

I didn't schedule or plan to have pacers at any point, so when people showed up it was a heart-warming surprise. My pacing support consisted of neighbors, firefighters and EMS workers, family, friends, co-workers and even complete strangers who had read or heard about the event through one of the many media outlets.

As the different pacers rotated in and out, the miles flew by quickly as the hot August Florida sun kicked into full gear. There were so many people that came and ran a surprising number of miles with me. There was one that really stood out though. Todd Thompson, a neighbor and firefighter EMT, showed up to run a few miles with me. This guy was a self-proclaimed "non-runner" who ended up covering approximately twenty-five miles with me completely out of the blue. His perseverance and determination to cover such distances was truly inspiring.

Even though the miles were flying by, I felt every inch of my course. The fact that I was running the same loop over and over added a unique sense of mental fatigue that I did not get to experience in the Keys. The 1.05-mile loop became absolutely mind-numbing. By mile thirty-one, I was completely sick of looking at the same homes in my neighborhood. If it was not for all the individuals who came out to talk to me and take my mind off the task at hand, I very well may have gone crazy with boredom.

It was at the mile forty marker that I realized that I was so distracted by the conversation of my pacers that I had forgotten to eat and drink. It wasn't long after my bleak realization that I crashed in a glorious display of self-destruction.

Here I was, forty miles into a one-hundred-mile run, and I had taken in hardly any meaningful calories or hydration. I stopped at my aid station and attempted to get some food into me while sipping on some water and electrolyte mix. I also thought it may be good to attempt to use the restroom, just to get a gauge on how dehydrated I was.

After a few moments of extreme focus, I finally gave up on the idea of producing any urine. I was almost twelve hours into the run, in ninety-degree weather with minimal shade, and needless to say, I was severely dehydrated and feeling every side effect of it. I finished the rest of my electrolyte drink and headed back out. Halfway around the next lap, my lower back and flank region started to cramp and throb. It felt as if my kidneys were turning themselves inside out. I cautiously finished off my lap and made the wise decision to rehydrate myself before continuing.

As I entered the aid station, Leigh-Ann asked what I

needed, as was the pattern after every lap. I told her that my back was hurting and that I needed water. She handed me a bottle, and I downed the entire contents within a few seconds. My body absorbed it like a sponge.

I told Leigh-Ann that I needed a lot more water and asked her to go inside and grab an unopened gallon. I told her that I needed to take the gallon with me on my next lap and finish it before returning. My plan was to just walk the next couple of miles and take it easy while my body recuperated. True to my word, the gallon was finished before I arrived back home. After walking about three miles and allowing the water to absorb while chasing it with electrolyte mix, I started to produce urine again.

I would be lying if I told you that I was not concerned by the sight and condition of my urine. It resembled the color of Coca-Cola with a red hue. It didn't take a doctor's diagnosis to know that this was bad. I decided to drink about another half a gallon of water and eat some food before returning to the course.

After about a ten- to fifteen-minute break, I felt the urge to return to the restroom. I was using empty sports drink bottles so that I could measure the amount and color. This time the liquid appeared more like urine and less like death in a bottle.

Once I had ingested some calories and got some more water into my system, I started to feel better. I made the decision to continue with the run under extreme caution. Rhabdomyolysis is a condition in which the kidneys start to break down and fail; anyone who participates in extreme endurance sports always has this concern lingering in the back of their mind. This was one nightmare that I did not want any part of.

In a strategic move to create accountability, I told my crew and everyone who was pacing me, including Todd, that I needed to stay on top of my water consumption and nutrition. Leigh-Ann was sure to drive the point home every time she saw me.

Making it to mile fifty was a huge accomplishment and mental checkpoint. Around this time, Todd finished off his twenty-fifth mile and had to go home to rest and get some sleep for his shift the next day. Even though his feet were blistered and his lower back was cramping, he stuck out those miles with me like a true champion. I am so grateful for the support that he showed, because that twenty-five-mile section of the run was one of the hardest and slowest portions.

As I continued on with my run, more and more fire and EMS crews arrived to show their support and complete a couple miles with me. Some guys even completed their miles while wearing their turn-out gear.

I know I have said this a lot, but it truly amazes me how willing people are to share their issues and struggles with someone who can relate. Some of the guys who ran with me were quiet, some joked around, and then there were a few that opened up about the pain in their lives. The miles shared with these firefighters made this experience one of the most meaningful events that I will probably ever run.

As the fire crews, family, friends and neighborhood support rotated in and out, the sun was starting to relent. Entering about mile seventy, the streetlights turned back on and the sun set. As the daylight faded into darkness, so did my energy.

My pace slowed significantly, and at this point I was pretty much running to a mailbox and walking to the next. I couldn't help but reflect on the early miles that I had completed when I first started running, back before I worked as a paramedic and when the weight of the world, my PTSD and addiction didn't crush me.

Here I was, struggling to make it mailbox to mailbox again, while picturing that young man who questioned his own potential. I drew strength knowing that the man I was today, the new man I had become, had the unwavering ability to complete whatever he set his mind to. With this undeniable absolute in mind, I continued to put one blistered foot in front of the other.

After about fifteen agonizingly slow miles, my body felt like it was back in the furnace at the Keys. Here I was, once again facing the deep, dark corners of my brain. Only this time I was doing so with confidence. My mind and body were falling apart, but my heart and spirit could not have been stronger.

Leigh-Ann saw the state I was in during those early hours of the morning, around mile eighty-five. I was stumbling my way through the course, hallucinating snakes on the road and talking to myself about only Lord knows what.

Leigh-Ann knew I needed company during the next few laps, and as usual she was right. It was a huge mental boost having my wife, best friend, key support and number one cheerleader accompany me into mile ninety.

During those laps, she continued to tell me how proud she was of me and how much she and Hannah looked up to me. Knowing that the two most important people in my life looked at me with admiration was healing for my soul. I had promised Leigh-Ann that when I became sober, I was going to change the person that I was and spend the rest of my life making up for my shortcomings.

Here I was, a completely different man, undergoing one of the most extreme displays of change and perseverance a person can take on. This run was not only to prove to myself that I wouldn't quit, but it was also to prove to my wife that I would see my decisions through to the end.

At mile ninety, I finally broke through the death grip. I was struck with a rogue bolt of energy, and somehow my broken legs and blistered feet found strength enough to return to running. Over the next four miles, I was able to pull off a nine- to ten-minute mile pace. As I flew around the course, I once again found thankfulness and gratitude in my heart. I thanked God for the distance he had brought me and the courage to carry on.

At mile ninety-four, I was still holding down a strong pace. It was just about sunrise as an older woman approached me on the course, dressed in exercise clothing. When she got closer, I could see that she had tears in her eyes, and she asked if I was the guy running the one hundred miles for mental health awareness.

I told her I was and introduced myself. As she tried to compose herself, she proceeded to tell me that her husband, who was in the Navy, had struggled with PTSD greatly. She told me that she couldn't run but was hoping that she could walk a few miles with me. My heart sank, not because of the disruption to my pace but because my cause was resonating with the community.

Upon completing three emotionally charged miles, I was at mile ninety-eight. I felt like this run was never going to end. As my walking pace came to a crawl, my brain started panicking at the insurmountable thought of completing another three miles.

After taking another agonizing forty minutes to complete mile ninety-eight, I turned the corner to see a fire engine sitting in front of my house. The crew was waiting to complete the race with me. I told them that I was barely moving and that at this pace it would take about an hour and a half to complete the final two miles.

The thought of moving that slowly didn't affect their motivation to complete this race with me at all. They decided that one of the guys would run with me while the other followed in the engine, in case they were to get a call. We started off in a death march as I screamed and cried internally. After making it about a quarter mile, the firefighter driving the engine started to play "Eye of the Tiger" over the P.A. system.

Now, anyone who has ever heard this song knows you do not walk to it. Again, from out of nowhere I was hit with a burst of strength. I started to shuffle my feet faster and faster until I was back to what could be considered running. I finished off mile ninety-nine and was now working on my final lap. As "Eye of the Tiger" was playing on repeat in the early morning air, my feet were on repeat as well. I repeatedly kept placing one foot in front of the other, and just like my theory dictates, doing this enough times will eventually bring the finish line to you.

Making the final turn onto my street, I burst into tears as I saw Leigh-Ann, Hannah and my mom waiting for me to film the finish. As I crossed my makeshift white chalk finish line, the firefighters congratulated me and thanked me for my service. After a few minutes of small talk, they pulled off, and I was once again standing at a finish line with my crew in full elation at my accomplishment. My heart and pride swelled as my brain digested the fact that this run solidified the truth that the KEYS 100 was not just a fluke or dumb luck.

The one-hundred-mile distance was ingrained in my soul. I was bursting at the seams with happiness. I wasn't just happy that I had finished; I was also ecstatic that I was experiencing the same joy that I had after my first one-hundred-mile completion.

Unlike drugs, the finish line didn't seem to have a diminishing return. If anything, this return was even stronger. As most addicts do, I planned to chase this feeling to see how strong it could become.

Part 2

6x12

The word "craving" is defined as, "a powerful desire for something."

As an addict in recovery, I am intimately connected with this word and its meaning. I spent many years of my life drinking myself into a drunken stupor and shooting opiates until my veins collapsed and became hardened knots in my arms and hands. I was familiar with the destructive nature of cravings, but I never knew how empowering and positive they could be. I learned over many miles that cravings, when used in a positive light, could actually yield drive and determination.

I now craved to become the best version of myself.

As with most addicts, I hit the ground running with my new focus, pun intended. I could not get enough of the ultra-community. After my one hundred-mile run around my neighborhood, that we affectionately dubbed "Race 2 Recovery", I signed up for multiple ultras in the upcoming months before the Daytona 100 in December.

I signed up for two 50Ks in October and the L.O.S.T 118, a one hundred and eighteen-mile trek around Lake Okeechobee, in February. Shortly after hearing about "Race 2 Recovery", the race director for Long Haul 100 reached out to me and invited me to take part in his one-hundred-mile race in January.

Being invited to a race is one of the greatest honors a race director can give someone, in my opinion. There was absolutely no way I could tell him, no, thank you.

After humbly accepting his invitation to attend Long Haul 100, I realized that my schedule was starting to become a bit intimidating. I was scheduled to complete the Daytona 100 in December, Long Haul 100 in January and L.O.S.T 118 in February. I was aiming to complete three one hundred-milers in sixty-three days. I knew I was biting off a lot, but I also knew the recipe to success: all I needed to do was continue putting one foot in front of another.

After completing the two 50Ks in October and the Space Coast Marathon in November, I found myself standing at the Jacksonville starting line of the 2019 Daytona 100. The plan was to start in Jacksonville and run one hundred miles south to Daytona Beach. This course is considered flat and "fast" … as "fast" as a one hundred-miler could be.

After huddling around at the six a.m. start, we were off. Running the first thirty-five miles of this race was an awesome experience. We passed scenic views of the Atlantic Ocean and ran directly in front of numerous million-dollar estates. The approximate twenty-mile stretch between mile ten-ish and thirty-ish was a little distressing. This stretch was in direct sunlight and ran on the shoulder of a busy two-lane ocean-front road. Just like the KEYS 100, where we ran on the shoulder of busy roadways, there was a bit of a "pucker factor" during this stretch.

At about mile thirty-two, I entered Historic St. Augustine, the nation's oldest city. Running through this area was unique. It was a busy section, with many visitors to the area that ran directly in front of the historic fort. Passing through, one cannot help but visualize all the history that took place there.

As I flew through the first fifty miles of this race, I set PRs for both my 50K and fifty-mile distance. I could not believe how great I felt as I breezed through the mile marker fifty aid station. Leigh-Ann and my family were crewing me as normal, but instead of meeting me every one to two miles, I was able to make it every four to five miles before needing their assistance.

After seeing how well I was doing, my crew decided to return to the hotel in St. Augustine to grab dinner and freshen up before settling in for what would turn out to be a long night.

Around mile sixty-one, my good fortune came to an end. After setting a third PR for the 100K distance, the wheels finally fell off. The fact that I had just completed sixty-one miles faster than I had ever completed them before finally caught up to me. My brain became hyper-aware of the blisters that had been forming on my feet. While everything below my waist was screaming in pain, my spirit did not falter; after all, this was now familiar and expected territory for me. The pain was almost welcome; we wouldn't want to make this one hundred-miler too easy, right?

After sending out a distress call to my crew, the cavalry finally showed up around mile sixty-eight with some fresh fluids, calories and a change of shoes and socks. Even though the supplies they brought to me were very much needed, their presence was the real game changer. I quickly went back to running shortly after they had arrived and taken care of my needs.

The stretch between miles seventy to eighty were my favorite miles of the course. This stretch was held alongside the ocean and its rolling waves. I turned my headphones off and ran through the darkness to the sound of crashing water. This section was so peaceful and tranquil, but as usual, there's always a calm before the storm when it comes to one hundred-milers.

Entering the mile eighty aid station, I was reduced to my signature death march. The next twenty miles would make up for the ease of the first eighty. I struggled to even keep a snail's pace as I made my way through Ormond Beach to Daytona. During this stretch, not only was I passed by other runners who appeared strong, but the sun also took to the sky and seemed to have a personal vendetta against me. I pretty much walked my way to mile ninety-five with one wobbly and painful step in front of another.

After checking in at the final aid station at mile ninety-five, I was completely over the race and just wanted it to be done. I dug deep and found the strength to return to a shuffle and trot. I cruised the last few miles of the course on the beach before returning to the residential neighborhood, where the finish line was waiting.

After crossing the finish line and posing for a few photos, we loaded up into our rented minivan and started the hour-and-a-half drive back to Central Florida.

The weeks seem to fly by on fast forward, because in the blink of an eye, there I was, toeing the line of Long Haul 100. My legs were still a little tight from the Daytona 100, and there were still soft spots on my feet from the previous blisters. Still, I showed up ready to put one foot in front of another.

Shortly after the start of the race, I found myself settling into a comfortable pace. This run would be my first official non-point-to-point race. I absolutely love the way Long Haul is set up! The race is comprised of three intersecting trail spurs that make up ten miles. The spurs meet at "tent city", the middle of the course, where runners and their crews set up their own personal aid stations and camp sites. This is also where the finish line and race headquarters are held. Every one-hundred-mile runner challenges themselves to complete ten full laps of spurs one, two and three.

I have run a bunch of great races, but Long Haul is definitely in a league of its own. Andy Mathews and his wife Amy do an amazing job with the planning and execution of this race. Andy is without a doubt one of the best race directors to ever put on a race. While there were some extremely impressive runners present and racing their hearts out, the overall vibe of the race was a giant party in the woods, in my experience. Andy had a DJ, loudspeakers, fog machines, laser lights and most importantly, top-tier volunteers. There was so much support and encouragement on this course, it was almost overwhelming. While I write the pages of this book, Long Haul 100 continues to be one of my absolute favorite races ever.

Even though this race is held on flat Florida trails, it is deceptively tough. As the only Western States 100 qualifying race in Florida, the trail, as expected, kicked my ass in the most glorious sense. Every lap of the spurs became progressively and significantly tougher than the last.

Since this was my first one hundred-miler on a trail instead of pavement, my blisters popped up notably faster. By mile forty, I had a deep throbbing blister on the bottom of my right foot. This little pain pocket was about the size of a silver dollar and seemed to be attached to every nerve in my entire foot. I tried multiple times to lance and pop it, but it was way too deep. I quickly accepted that this blister was part of my life and that I was powerless to change it. I reminded myself that to my knowledge, nobody has ever died from a foot blister. I chuckled to myself as I thought, *it's a good thing your feet are so far away from your heart.*

I returned to the course and returned to putting one foot in front of the other.

As the day turned to night, I was able to witness the amazing sunset through the lens of the woods. I watched as the forest line created a picturesque silhouette of the vibrant oranges and reds that spread across the sky. During this time, all was right in my world. I didn't even focus on how bad my foot felt. I was just beyond thankful to be there and to be able to witness such beauty. The sunset was just what I needed to remind myself of just how insignificant my problems were and shift my thinking to gratitude, which is where it needed to be.

Over the next couple of laps, I fell into a strong groove and pace. I was maintaining a very consistent run–walk approach that seemed to be propelling me well. As with all my races, I used the miles and suffering to meet and bond with the other runners around me. Another aspect that I loved about this course was the fact that I was never too far away from another runner but not close enough to feel cramped.

One of my favorite parts about races is meeting new people and learning what motivates them. It astonishes me to learn the depths of individual drive in other runners. Around mile eighty-ish of Long Haul, I ended up pacing with two other runners, Bernadette and Adam. Both were sitting right next to me on the struggle bus. Bernadette was holding down a walking pace that was just as fast as my run.

After exchanging pleasantries and agreeing on the difficulty of this race, Bernadette went on to tell me about some of her running adventures, including her three successful finishes of the Vol State 500K, a three hundred and fourteen-mile run across Tennessee. I was awestruck by the thought of a three hundred and fourteen-mile race. The conversation with them helped adjust my perspective and pull me out of the little pity party that I had unknowingly slipped into. After about five to six miles together, the three of us ended up separating, as most runners will do over long-distance races. I was so thankful for their conversation and company, and I found myself fully invested in their success and finish.

There's a magic in one hundred-mile races that reveals the best in humanity. While these events are first and foremost a competition and race, I have never met another participant who does not want every other runner on the course to finish.

After dealing with the worst of mankind for so many years as a paramedic, I can honestly and solely thank the ultra-community for completely restoring my faith in humanity.

Entering my final lap at mile ninety, I was a broken man. My legs were Jell-O, and my mind was once again completely unraveled. I was hallucinating snakes on the trail and shadow dogs running through the woods. My final ten miles were excruciating; every uneven foot strike on the trail was torture, not only to my feet but to my entire body.

Making my way out of the woods to tent city, I probably resembled Tom Hanks from *Castaway*. I was filthy and thoroughly delusional. The only thing that kept me from becoming best friends with a volleyball was the fact that I did not have one present. I did however become very acquainted with multiple rocks and roots along the trail, as I tripped and stumbled my way through the final lap.

Approaching the finish line, my crew was waiting in excited anticipation. Hannah ran to me once I was in view. Then she and I completed the last fifty yards, running hand in hand. Reflecting on the moment, we both had huge smiles on our faces. As was customary, when in the presence of my crew, it was hard to feel anything but joy.

Crossing the finish line was once again an incredible experience. As I had hoped, the feelings of success and gratitude were even stronger than my previous finishes. I loved this feeling; I was earning my self-respect back, one painful step at a time.

After making it back home, I crashed. My body and mind were thoroughly and comprehensively exhausted. After waking up after my first full rest, I lay in bed, basking in my triumph. I replayed all the things in the race that had gone well and not so well, in my head. I relaxed with a smile on my face. *I did it*, I had earned my fourth one-hundred-mile buckle. The shelf that I kept them on started to get crowded – this was a good problem to have.

I allowed myself to digest my success before being yanked back to reality. I was promptly humbled by the fact that in three weeks I would be running one hundred and eighteen miles while attempting the L.O.S.T 118. I tried to imagine how tough it would be to complete another eighteen miles on my current feet. I only spent about three seconds pondering this horror before taking my negative and anxious thoughts captive. I quickly discarded them and refocused on the only thing I needed to be worried about,

Once again, putting one foot in front of another.

Now, there are a lot of difficult things in this world, things that will altogether dismantle you before grinding you into sand. In my life experience, I would place the L.O.S.T 118 near the very top of this list. Standing at the starting line, I had little to no idea just how difficult this run would be. There was no way for me to know at this time that this course was about to chew me up and spit me out.

The L.O.S.T 118 was held on the Lake Okeechobee Scenic Trail, a one hundred and eighteen-mile single loop of Lake Okeechobee in south Florida, held primarily on the rocky dike around the lake.

The race director, George Maxwell, while being a great guy, was a hardened ultrarunner himself. He was of the "old school" persuasion. He created his race with zero course support in the form of aid stations and required every runner to rely solely on themselves and their crew. At the beginning of this race, I was extremely grateful that I was starting with the confidence of four other one hundred-mile finishes under my belt and the best crew anyone could hope for.

However, I was not grateful for the I.T. band issues and partially healed blisters that lingered from Long Haul, which had taken place only three weeks earlier.

After starting, I quickly slipped into my conservative and safe pace. I played leapfrog with other runners who were also trying to pace themselves as sensibly as they could.

I ended up catching up to a group of familiar faces and slipped into their group. Among the familiar faces were Andy Mathews and Bernadette, as well as a couple of other friendly runners. Andy was running the race as part of a relay team, while Bernadette was attempting the full one hundred and eighteen miles. We laughed and joked for the first six to seven miles as the distance flew by.

After the first crewing point, the group dispersed and separated, as standard for these types of events. Bernadette and

I found ourselves still running the same pace and ended up sticking together until around mile eighteen, when I had to take about twenty minutes to address the blisters that were already bleeding.

Once I got my feet as squared away as possible, I jumped back onto the course and started chipping away at the overwhelming distance, one step at a time.

I found myself running alone with a semi-strong walk–run pace until around mile twenty-five, when I noticed another runner at the crewing spot struggling to keep food down. As I watched him struggle, I knew he was panicking internally. I knew how difficult of a spot that was and my heart went out to him.

As I started to head back to the course after completing my crew stop, I swung by his vehicle and introduced myself. He said his name was Bryan and that this was his first organized one hundred-mile attempt. I asked if he wanted to chisel away some miles with me. Both he and his single crew member looked relieved to have some company. As we started making our way down the course, we slipped into conversation very easily.

Bryan and I discussed many topics for the next twenty-five miles that we spent together, everything from religion and spirituality to politics and music. As we approached mile forty-five, I knew he was starting to slip. I heard the slight shift in his tone from optimism to pessimism.

One of the greatest lessons I have learned during long-distance running is that attitude is everything.

One small negative thought has a way of snowballing and picking up momentum until it's all you can focus on. Negative thoughts during a one hundred-miler are cancerous and must be dealt with swiftly and precisely.

I tried my very best to keep the positivity flowing and his attention on the next steps. Unfortunately, it was too late. Once we reached mile fifty, we took a short three to four minute break to meet with our crews.

As I was walking back to the dike after meeting with my crew, I swung by his vehicle. I found him sitting in the passenger seat with his eyes closed. I told him it was time to get a move on and that we needed to get back to it. He told me that he just needed two to three more minutes and that he would catch up to me shortly. That was the last time I would see him. He ended up dropping shortly after I returned to the course. Now, I was running completely alone. Other than Bryan, I had not seen another runner since mile eighteen when Bernadette and I separated.

As I ran under the bright moonlight, I didn't even need my headlamp. It was a pretty cool experience running on that dike with the moonlight dancing on the lake.

As I continued to push forward, Leigh-Ann and my crew planned to meet me around mile fifty-five for the last crew stop of the night. After two sketchy drives from the finish line at the KEYS 100 and the Daytona 100, I had promised that Leigh-Ann would never have to drive that tired again. We planned to have her stop for the night at a hotel in Okeechobee to get plenty of rest before crewing the next day.

After meeting for the final time and returning to the course, I felt pretty strong. I had my second wind and was ready mentally to run the night portion uncrewed.

As I made my way up the dike, I noticed a set of purple anal beads laying on the side of the trail. I chuckled out loud and took a picture. I have run into many funny and weird things on trails since I started running, but this was by far one of the funniest and most unexpected. I probably would not have laughed so hard if I had realized at the time that this would be an omen for the rest of my night.

Miles fifty to seventy were some of the loneliest miles I have ever run in my life. I found myself hyper-aware of the fact that I was completely alone in the darkness. I tried to think about all the positives that had happened during this race, but I had a very difficult time refocusing due to the small number of things that actually did go well.

I was spelunking deep in the pain cave. My feet and legs were throbbing as I passed the halfway mark around mile sixty-ish. I felt the familiar pain of running on broken glass, as every nerve in my feet and legs was on high alert. My hips were tight and restricted my pace, as my back twinged and cramped. My shoulders and neck ached while patiently waiting, ready to pounce in spasm if I extended my range of motion even slightly.

Around mile sixty-four, the hallucinations really became an issue. The main problem was not being able to tell the difference between hallucinations and real life. I would visualize cars driving in my direction and bears walking and running on the trail in front of me. My eyes struggled to focus on the potential threat, as they always just flirted with my line of sight, which was restricted by the darkness. I turned on my headlamp to get a better look, to no avail.

Around mile seventy, I caught up with another one of the runners on the course named Casey. I am so grateful that I did, because if it weren't for him, I would have missed a critical turn and run, Lord knows how far, off course.

After a few miles of much-needed conversation, he stopped

to rest with his crew for a few minutes, and he asked me multiple times if I needed anything before, we parted ways. I thankfully accepted some soda and gummies before moving forward. I knew if I stopped for any amount of time, there was a high likelihood that I would not get back up. Casey and I would end up leapfrogging each other for the next thirty miles, constantly checking in with each other to make sure that we were both holding it together.

As the sun took to the sky around mile ninety, I struggled to keep from breaking down emotionally. I was completely crippled by my weariness and exhaustion. I had fallen asleep multiple times while putting one foot in front of the other, only to be jarred awake by my impact on the loose, rocky course. I can clearly remember thinking, *yep, here I go again*, as I fell asleep while moving.

Just as I reached my breaking point while sitting on the side of the trail draining blisters and retaping my feet, my phone rang. I broke down crying when I saw my wife's name flashing on my caller I.D. as I answered. Her sweet and rested voice was exactly what I needed to pull me out of the rut I was in and provide a burst of energy.

I told her about the hellacious night of hallucinations, exhaustion, and the multiple falls. She expressed concern through a tone of admiration and respect. I caught her up on everything I would need at the next crewing point around mile eighty-two. I quickly gave up on trying to drain and tape the blisters on the bottoms and sides of my feet and replaced my socks and shoes. I wanted to capitalize on my newfound energy and get to that crewing point as quickly as possible to see them.

After spending most of my night wallowing in isolation

and self-pity delusions, I NEEDED TO SEE MY FAMILY'S FACES!

Shortly after getting back up to carry on, my legs buckled in response to the pain fiesta happening in my socks. My feet were throwing in the white towel and telling my brain, "NO MORE!"

I stumbled as I tried to keep myself upright. I screamed out loud in frustration and pain. In a reactive display of bitterness, I stomped my foot as hard as I could on the rocky course. My thin trail shoes offered little cushion as my blistered foot slammed into the sharp, jagged rocks.

My brain was shocked that the foot was not met with an outpouring of pain but of instant relief. I could feel a wetness soaking into my sock and knew the most problematic blister on my right foot, the same one that I had struggled with at Long Haul, had burst and filled my sock with serum and blood. The alleviation was instant and heavenly; it was much needed after a night from hell.

After meeting my family and spending some much-needed reunion minutes with them, I was off again. I was completely sick of the course at this point. There is not much to look at on the dike around Lake Okeechobee, and the lack of scenery created a daunting mental aspect that made this race especially difficult. It didn't matter though; I had my crew back and their smiling and cheerful faces were the only scenery I needed. We went back to our normal crewing strategy as I continued to tackle the course, one step at a time.

Entering mile one hundred proved to create mixed emotions. On one hand, I was proud that I had made it this far on my broken feet. On the other hand, I couldn't help but think that I should be done, and that these last eighteen miles were complete BS.

At mile one hundred I had to climb up the steep embankment back to the dike trail, after exiting shortly for a section on the shoulder of the road. As I climbed up the sharp grade, my feet slipped. I was able to catch myself before slipping back down but in doing so clenched my jaw and teeth. I felt a quick pop in my mouth and a stabbing pain in my jaw to follow. My tongue instantly investigated the scene of the pop, in a cautious manner. I was horrified, as the pain did not subside, and my tongue reported back with its findings.

I had BROKEN one of my bottom molars on my right side!

Of course, this had to happen; it was as if the universe looked at me and said, "You know what? Richard looks pretty good right now. How can I shake things up? Oh, I know… let's break one of his teeth, with eighteen God-forsaken miles to go!"

I quickly spit out the broken half of my tooth and rinsed the blood out of my mouth. Even though it seemed like this was it and I would have no choice but to stop, I didn't dwell on it for too long. I relieved my brain from its duties of decision making and placed myself on autopilot, while I continued to place one foot in front of the other.

Upon making it to mile one hundred and five, I realized that the stinging razor-sharp tooth pain was not getting worse. Don't get me wrong, it was bad… just not getting worse. Honestly, I'm not sure it could have become worse if it tried. I reminded myself that if I quit, I would still be in pain. I told myself that I might as well get a buckle out of the ordeal. I stood firm on the fact that I had not come this far, to only come this far.

I put my head down and only focused on the upcoming steps as I wrestled with the final thirteen miles of that bear of a course. I was reduced to a zombie walk as I crawled my way to the finish line.

As I approached the final turn to the finish, I was about a half mile away. I could make out my family waiting for me in the distance. My wife called me with excited tears in her voice. She praised me for making it as Hannah screamed and shouted for me in the background. I asked if they would start walking in my direction to meet me for the final few yards.

By the time we met, I could see the finish line. My eyes welled with tears of both pride and pain. As we made our way up the final climb, George, the race director, was standing there waiting for me, belt buckle in hand.

After shaking my hand and awarding me my buckle, I found out that I had won the "DFL" bragging rights. For anyone who isn't familiar with racing abbreviations, "DFL" stands for "Dead Fucking Last". Out of the twenty-some people who had started the race as solo runners, only ten of us had finished. I was proudly standing here as the tenth place finisher and couldn't have been prouder of myself.

For me, these types of events are not about placing myself on a podium but elevating myself in my own eyes. I was on a mission to earn my self-respect back one step at a time, and I would continue to push myself, even if it was at a snail's pace. This race was mind-breakingly difficult, but it did not hold a candle to the difficulty I would have faced while looking in the mirror if I had chosen to throw in the towel. I was leaving this race with a broken tooth and jacked up feet, but my spirit was fully intact.

After arriving home and having a much-needed root canal on my broken tooth and catching up on rest, I felt amazing. I was truly stunned by my ability to complete three races of this distance within sixty-three days. I was a man on fire. I was looking forward to testing and stretching my self-perceived limitations and flirting with the boundaries of my potential, wherever those may be.

Roughly one month after my L.O.S.T 118 finish, the entire world was shaken to its core as we all found ourselves stretching our self-perceived limitations. Covid-19 hit the earth like a freight train, stopping everyone in their tracks.

As the entire world seemed to shut down, races were no exception. In the blink of the eye, it seemed that every scheduled race was cancelled overnight. Obviously, races are very low on the priority list when it comes to safety and preservation of human life. Although the need and reason to cancel events was obvious, it was still painful to watch all my therapy sessions being terminated.

After a few weeks of immature self-pity over my cancelled events, it dawned on me that nobody was keeping me from running. As long as I practiced all the recommended safety standards from the experts, I felt confident in returning to my road-based therapy sessions.

I perused Google for creative ideas and ways to keep me motivated, and to my pleasant surprise I found that there were organized one hundred-mile races that were being held virtually. These would allow me to feel some connection to my tribe while still attending my healing appointments.

After signing up for two virtual one hundred-milers, I noticed that if I played my cards right, I would be able to celebrate my one-year anniversary of completing the KEYS 100 by running my sixth one hundred-miler. So, that is exactly what I did. To complete this goal, I would need to run the two one hundred-milers over the upcoming three months.

On May 16, 2020, three days before my one-year anniversary of my first one-hundred-mile finish, I found myself crossing another makeshift finish line in front of my house, just as I had one month earlier in April for my fifth triple digit finish.

As I stood in my front yard, reflecting on the year of my crazy running events, I chuckled internally. Here I was, adding my sixth finisher buckle to my shelf, when only a year ago I was demanding that I would never attempt another one. Life has a funny way of unfolding when you allow it to. I went from someone who could not bear to look into a mirror to someone who held his head high. It was a long and difficult year with many challenges and obstacles, but through constant perseverance and only focusing on the next steps, I was able to fight and claw my way back to being someone who respected himself.

Even though running six one hundred-mile runs in twelve months seems like a lot, I know it's only the tip of the iceberg that is my potential. I look forward to exploring my boundaries and savoring the journey one step at a time. From what I hear, Death Valley sounds lovely in July.

Part 3

No Finish Line

I read somewhere once that "all great change is preceded by chaos". It is a funny thought to think that the hell that I endured with my depression, anxiety, PTSD, anger, substance abuse, alcoholism and suicidal thoughts could possibly be used for good. I have learned a lot of things in my life, mostly the hard way. One of the life lessons that has been ingrained in my brain is that any stumbling blocks that the whirlwind of life throws at you can be turned into steppingstones given the right amount of work.

If you would have told me at the age of twenty-six that I would be where I am today, I would have laughed in your face. If you asked that same version of me where I would see myself in the future my answer probably would have been, "Dead."

Over the course of my life, I was slowly broken down by stresses and traumas that no human should have to endure. I have borne witness to some of the worst that humanity has to offer. I have experienced bullying first-hand and can testify to the destructive impact that it can have on a young and developing mind and self-esteem.

I have survived the mental anguish of severe depression, crippling anxiety, explosive anger and a sincere desire to want to die. I was familiar with the short-lived love, romance and escape of drugs and alcohol. I found myself no longer living life but simply existing in a state of numbness and remorse.

One of the most frustrating aspects of living with mental health issues is never truly being able to put a finger on what exactly is wrong. You find yourself living your life knowing that you are unhappy but having no idea of how to restore the happiness and remove the unyielding sadness.

Like a resilient rock on the shoreline exposed to the tide and the relentless beating of waves, life has a way of pounding even the strongest of us into a pile of washed-out rubble. Even though not everyone struggles with mental health issues, low self-esteem or substance abuse, most of us know what it is like to struggle and have life kick us in the teeth.

One of the most important things to remember is that you can't always help the stress that life throws at you. Though, through drive and determination you can learn healthy and constructive ways to react to it.

If I could choose to impart one piece of hard-earned wisdom to everyone struggling, I would choose to share that it is okay to ask for help. Sometimes the most courageous act one can do is to admit that they are struggling and extend a hand for assistance.

After many years of hovering inches over rock bottom, I finally kissed it. I found myself in one of the darkest holes that my mind could imagine. I was failing at life, and after failing at death, I knew I needed help. I felt worthless and like I didn't even deserve hope. I hated myself and avoided the man in the mirror at all costs.

Just like a wildfire has a destructive force to destroy a forest, mental health issues have a destructive tendency of leaving someone's life black, bleak and barren. While it is hard to see it at the time, there is no greater potential for regrowth. In my case, my regrowth was stronger and more lush than I could have ever imagined.

I found redemption in one of the most unlikely places – inside a pair of running shoes. After running from myself my entire life, I made the bold decision that any of us can make, and I decided to change direction.

Most of my important life lessons came to me while on the run. I learned patience, discipline, and perseverance, but more importantly, I learned forgiveness.

I learned how to forgive myself for all the destructive decisions that I had made in my life. I was reintroduced to the man in the mirror, a man that I respected.

I learned to have patience with myself and realize that it is okay to make mistakes, as long as you learn from them and adjust accordingly.

I learned true discipline and what it meant to give yourself entirely to a goal and to not stop until you reach it, no matter how broken and exhausted you may feel.

I learned perseverance, and I realized that there is no finish line when it comes to self-improvement. Also, I was taught that I could overcome any and all obstacles that life chose to throw at me, as long as I continued to place one foot in front of the other.

For me, running was not just an exercise, a weekend excursion or finisher award on a wall… it was my redemption, my rebirth… my recovery!

Printed by BoD™in Norderstedt, Germany